30.42

D1564277

# Gun Control

# Other books in the Issues on Trial Series

Affirmative Action

Education

Euthanasia

Free Speech

Homosexuality

Immigration

Religious Liberty

Women's Rights

# Gun Control

*Justin Karr, Book Editor*

**GREENHAVEN PRESS**
*A part of Gale, Cengage Learning*

Detroit • New York • San Francisco • New Haven, Conn • Waterville, Maine • London

Christine Nasso, *Publisher*
Elizabeth Des Chenes, *Managing Editor*

© 2007 Greenhaven Press, a part of Gale, Cengage Learning.

*For more information, contact:*
Greenhaven Press
27500 Drake Rd.
Farmington Hills, MI 48331-3535
Or you can visit our Internet site at gale.cengage.com

ISBN-13: 978-0-7377-3806-3
ISBN-10: 0-7377-3806-5

Library of Congress Control Number: 2007932773

Printed in the United States of America
2 3 4 5 6 7 12 11 10 09 08

# Contents

Foreword                                                                  11

Introduction                                                              14

## Chapter 1: Can the States Prohibit Citizens from Keeping and Bearing Arms?

Case Overview: *Presser v. Illinois* (1886)                               22

1. The Court's Decision: States Can                                       24
   Control and Regulate Private Military
   Groups and Associations
   *Justice William Burnham Woods*

   The Supreme Court unanimously upheld as constitutional a state statute that forbade groups from associating
   together as military organizations without a license. Reaffirming that the Second Amendment limits only the federal government and not the states, the *Presser v. Illinois*
   Court further stated that states could not "prohibit the
   people from keeping and bearing arms, so as to deprive
   the United States of their rightful resource for maintaining public security."

2. Limits on the Power of States to                                       30
   Regulate Firearms
   *Regina McClendon*

   A legal researcher examines the objections to gun control
   legislation that have been raised in California, centering
   on the constitutional rights and prohibitions of national
   and state governments addressed in *Presser*.

3. The Second Amendment Does Not                                          38
   Apply to the States
   *Stephen P. Halbrook*

   A lawyer and philosophy scholar introduces the *Presser*
   case in its historical context, addressing the Court's assertion at the time that the Bill of Rights does not directly apply to the states.

4. Anti-Gun Lobbyists Take the Supreme     50
Court's Decision Out of Context
*Dave Kopel*

A writer at the forefront of the gun-control debate claims that *Presser* is the most significant gun case from the nineteenth century, one that is inappropriately cited by anti-gun groups as supporting the notion of a ban on guns.

5. The Supreme Court's Attempt to     55
Nullify the Second Amendment
*Bob Butler*

A computer scientist and gun-rights enthusiast predicts that if *Presser* were heard today, the Court would find the state of Illinois in violation of the First and Fourteenth Amendments, though he acknowledges that the Court has not yet contradicted the verdict.

## Chapter 2: The Supreme Court Addresses the Second Amendment

Case Overview: *United States v. Miller* (1939)     60

1. The Court's Decision: The National Firearms     62
Act Does Not Violate the Constitution
*Justice James Clark McReynolds*

In a unanimous ruling, the Supreme Court determined that the National Firearms Act of 1934, which required that certain types of firearms be registered with the Miscellaneous Tax Unit, was not in conflict with the Second Amendment. The Supreme Court ruled that the Second Amendment does not guarantee the right to keep and bear short-barreled shotguns and machine guns.

2. The Fallacy of the Revisionist Approach to     70
Gun Rights
*David Yassky*

A law professor contends that the *Miller* verdict "plainly rule out the revisionists' Libertarian Approach" to the Second Amendment, citing the inertia of the courts on gun-rights issues as proof that *Miller* does not provide the foundation for an individual-rights interpretation of the Second Amendment.

3. The Protection of an Individual's                    **81**
   Right to Keep and Bear Arms
   *Brannon P. Denning and Glenn H. Reynolds*

   Two law professors counter Yassky's argument concerning
   the *Miller* case, asserting that the case "does not close the
   door on the enforcement of the Second Amendment."

4. Gun-Control Measures Support the Court's             **93**
   Interpretation of the Second Amendment
   *Amitai Etzioni*

   A critic in favor of gun control suggests that the country
   should rely on *Miller* and 125 years of case law that supports the constitutionality of restricting gun ownership by
   private citizens.

5. Second Amendment Scholarship and the                **97**
   Individual Rights Interpretation
   *Jerry Bonanno*

   A law school graduate surveys the range of scholarship
   interpreting the Second Amendment, focusing on the
   *Miller* case as the Supreme Court's most explicit discussion of the right to keep and bear arms.

## Chapter 3: Are Gun Manufacturers Liable for Negligence?

Case Overview: *Hamilton v. Beretta* (2001)               **113**

1. The Court's Decision: Handgun Manufacturers         **116**
   Are Not Liable
   *Judge Richard C. Wesley*

   In *Hamilton v. Beretta*, the Second Circuit Court of Appeals held that handgun manufacturers do not owe a duty
   of reasonable care, in terms of the marketing and distribution of their products, to people who have been injured
   or killed through illegally obtained firearms. The court
   also ruled that the defendants could not be held liable
   under the theory of negligent entrustment, and that liability based on market share could not apply to gun manufacturers.

2. The Significance of the Suits Against        127
   Gun Makers
   *Daniel M. Duval, et al.*

   Cornell University Law School students discuss the
   *Hamilton* verdict, focusing on the case's effect on the notion that the gun industry has a duty to exercise reasonable care in marketing and distributing firearms.

3. An Upset to Gun-Control Advocates        134
   *Erich Pratt*

   The Gun Owners of America's director of communications comments on the *Hamilton* decision from the assumed perspective of his opponents, the gun-control advocates.

4. Negligence Suits Against Gun        138
   Manufacturers Denied
   *Frank J. Giliberti*

   A product liability lawyer details the relevant issues of
   the *Hamilton* case, addressing the question of duty and
   assessing the impact of the court's decision.

5. The Federal Law Shielding Gun        145
   Manufacturers from Lawsuits
   *David Dean*

   A law student analyzes the 2005 Protection of Lawful
   Commerce in Arms Act, a federal law designed to end
   lawsuits such as *Hamilton*, in which plaintiffs attempted
   to prove the negligent behavior of gun makers.

6. Congress Was Justified in Passing the        150
   Protection of Lawful Commerce in Arms Act
   *Charley Reese*

   A veteran journalist and National Rifle Association member argues in support of the federal law to protect gun
   manufacturers from civil liability lawsuits like *Hamilton*.

7. An Overview of the Suits Against        154
   Gun Manufacturers
   *Mireia Artigot i Golobardes*

   A law student provides a summary of the legal theories
   behind the lawsuits filed against gun makers and comments on Congress's legislative action in 2005.

# Chapter 4: Maintaining the Right to Keep and Bear Arms

Case Overview: *United States v. Emerson* (2001)     **168**

1. The Court's Decision: The Second Amendment Applies to Individuals     **171**
*Judge William Garwood*

The Fifth Circuit Court of Appeals ruled in *United States v. Emerson* that the Second Amendment protects, but does not unconditionally guarantee, an individual's right to keep and bear arms. The court ruled that this right is subject to "limited, narrowly tailored specific exceptions," and that federal gun-control laws do not violate the Constitution in specific situations such as the circumstances in question in the *Emerson* case.

2. Concurring Opinion: Whether the Right to Bear Arms Is an Individual or Collective Right Is of No Consequence in This Case     **183**
*Judge Robert M. Parker*

One of the three circuit judges for the *Emerson* case submits a specially concurring opinion in which he argues that the court should have avoided discussing the constitutional issue concerning the right to keep and bear arms because it was not necessary to decide this case.

3. The Limits Placed on Gun Control     **187**
*Michael C. Dorf*

A law professor discusses the reasoning behind *Emerson* and its potential effect on future gun-control laws, maintaining that while the court's opinion is well-researched, a convincing historical case could also be made in favor of a collective rights interpretation of the Second Amendment.

4. The Fifth Circuit Disregarded                           196
   Contemporary Issues, Focusing Solely on
   the 1789 Constitutional Text
   *Akhil and Vikram Amar*

   Two legal scholars assert that the Fifth Circuit "told the
   wrong constitutional story" in the *Emerson* ruling, high-
   lighting omissions in the court's methodology.

5. The Court Did Not Err in Its Analysis                   203
   *Stephen P. Halbrook*

   An attorney argues against the Amar brothers' interpretation of the *Emerson* ruling, describing it as inappropriately critical of the court's historical reasoning and unre-
   alistic in its expectations of the court's analysis.

Organizations to Contact                                    209

For Further Research                                        214

Index                                                       219

# Foreword

The U.S. courts have long served as a battleground for the most highly charged and contentious issues of the time. Divisive matters are often brought into the legal system by activists who feel strongly for their cause and demand an official resolution. Indeed, subjects that give rise to intense emotions or involve closely held religious or moral beliefs lay at the heart of the most polemical court rulings in history. One such case was *Brown v. Board of Education* (1954), which ended racial segregation in schools. Prior to *Brown*, the courts had held that blacks could be forced to use separate facilities as long as these facilities were equal to that of whites.

For years many groups had opposed segregation based on religious, moral, and legal grounds. Educators produced heartfelt testimony that segregated schooling greatly disadvantaged black children. They noted that in comparison to whites, blacks received a substandard education in deplorable conditions. Religious leaders such as Martin Luther King Jr. preached that the harsh treatment of blacks was immoral and unjust. Many involved in civil rights law, such as Thurgood Marshall, called for equal protection of all people under the law, as their study of the Constitution had indicated that segregation was illegal and un-American. Whatever their motivation for ending the practice, and despite the threats they received from segregationists, these ardent activists remained unwavering in their cause.

Those fighting against the integration of schools were mainly white southerners who did not believe that whites and blacks should intermingle. Blacks were subordinate to whites, they maintained, and society had to resist any attempt to break down strict color lines. Some white southerners charged that segregated schooling was *not* hindering blacks' education. For example, Virginia attorney general J. Lindsay Almond asserted, "With the help and the sympathy and the love and respect of the white people of the South, the colored man has risen under that educational process to a place of eminence and respect throughout the nation. It has served him well." So when the Supreme Court ruled against the segregationists in *Brown*, the South responded with vociferous cries of protest. Even government leaders criticized the decision. The governor of Arkansas, Orval Faubus, stated that he would not "be a party to any attempt to force acceptance of change to which the people are so overwhelmingly opposed." Indeed, resistance to integration was so great that when black students arrived at the formerly all-white Central High School in Arkansas, federal troops had to be dispatched to quell a threatening mob of protesters.

Nevertheless, the *Brown* decision was enforced and the South integrated its schools. In this instance, the Court, while not settling the issue to everyone's satisfaction, functioned as an instrument of progress by forcing a major social change. Historian David Halberstam observes that the *Brown* ruling "deprived segregationist practices of their moral legitimacy. . . . It was therefore perhaps the single most important moment of the decade, the moment that separated the old order from the new and helped create the tumultuous era just arriving." Considered one of the most important victories for civil rights, *Brown* paved the way for challenges to racial segregation in many areas, including on public buses and in restaurants.

In examining *Brown*, it becomes apparent that the courts play an influential role—and face an arduous challenge—in shaping the debate over emotionally charged social issues. Judges must balance competing interests, keeping in mind the high stakes and intense emotions on both sides. As exemplified by *Brown*, judicial decisions often upset the status quo and initiate significant changes in society. Greenhaven Press's Issues on Trial series captures the controversy surrounding influential court rulings and explores the social ramifications of such decisions from varying perspectives. Each anthology highlights one social issue—such as the death penalty, students' rights, or wartime civil liberties. Each volume then focuses on key historical and contemporary court cases that helped mold the issue as we know it today. The books include a compendium of primary sources—court rulings, dissents, and immediate reactions to the rulings—as well as secondary sources from experts in the field, people involved in the cases, legal analysts, and other commentators opining on the implications and legacy of the chosen cases. An annotated table of contents, an in-depth introduction, and prefaces that overview each case all provide context as readers delve into the topic at hand. To help students fully probe the subject, each volume contains book and periodical bibliographies, a comprehensive index, and a list of organizations to contact. With these features, the Issues on Trial series offers a well-rounded perspective on the courts' role in framing society's thorniest, most impassioned debates.

# Introduction

In the gun-control debate, the opposing sides agree on very few issue-related statements. Perhaps the one exception is this: the prevention of gun violence against, and by, children and teenagers in the United States is of utmost importance.

The report *Protect Children, Not Guns 2007* from the Children's Defense Fund notes the following statistics: 2,825 children and teenagers—both boys and girls, representing races, ethnicities, backgrounds, and religions across the spectrum—died in 2004 as a result of gun violence, which represents "more than the total number of American service men and women who died in combat in Iraq and Afghanistan since those wars began in 2003 through December 2006." This breaks down to the deaths of almost 8 children or teens per day and 235 per month. In 2004, the organization stresses, "57 law enforcement officers were killed in the line of duty" while "58 *preschoolers* were killed by firearms." Furthermore, the Fund reports that for every child and teenager who dies from a gunshot wound, there are four or five additional nonfatal injuries.

While recognizing the importance of gun safety and protecting children from firearms, the National Rifle Association (NRA) offers information on gun-related deaths among children from a different perspective in its 2007 *Firearm Safety in America* report: Since 1930, the document indicates, the annual number of accidental deaths from firearms has decreased 80%, even though the U.S. population has more than doubled and the number of firearms has quintupled. Accidental shooting deaths among children, the report states, have decreased 89% since 1975, and are currently at an all-time annual low. The NRA also emphasizes that firearms are only responsible for .6% of accidental deaths per year in America. The organization further stresses that among children, accidental gun-related deaths fall behind fatalities due to motor vehicles (45%), suffocation (18%), drowning (14%), fires (9%), bicycles and tricycles (2%), poisoning (2%), falls (2%), environmental factors (2%), and medical mistakes (1%). As statistics from opposing sides of the gun-control debate demonstrate, gun-rights groups prefer to focus their analysis of the issue on the reduced frequency of gun-related fatalities among minors in recent years, while gun-control advocates highlight the sheer number of unnecessary deaths due to firearms in the United States. Although gun-rights groups characterize some of the studies cited by gun-control advocates as flawed and vice versa, the opponents nevertheless concur that an aggressive effort to eliminate gun violence among America's youth is needed. They disagree, however, on how to achieve that goal.

## Guns in the Home

Despite all the media attention to school shootings in recent years, the majority of firearm-related deaths of children and teens occurs not in the school, but in the home. A study published in the *Archives of Pediatric & Adolescent Medicine* in 1999, which set out to "determine the ownership and usual storage location of firearms used in unintentional and self-inflicted intentional firearm deaths and injuries" in children and adolescents, found that in 65% of suicides and suicide attempts by adolescents, the guns used were owned by a member of the victim's household—57% of the time by the parents themselves. The gun used belonged to a household member in 23% of unintentional injuries and deaths as well.

Given these numbers, some professionals cite the proliferation of guns in homes as a major contributor to U.S. gun violence among children and teens. It is estimated that 35% or more of U.S. homes with children contain at least one gun (and more than one gun is present in 69% of these, according to the 2001 *RAND Health Research Highlights*), and a September 2005 study by the Centers for Disease Control and Prevention revealed that "more than 1.7 million children live in homes with loaded, unlocked guns," as reported by Sandra G. Boodman in her 2006 *Washington Post* article entitled "In Harm's Way: Guns and Kids." The 2001 RAND analysis of the ways guns are stored in U.S. homes with children determined that "fewer than half [of U.S. families with children] store their firearms unloaded, locked, and away from ammunition," which is widely recommended.

## CAP Laws

A study conducted by Frances Baxley and Matthew Miller and published in 2006 in the *Archives of Pediatric & Adolescent Medicine*, which surveyed, separately, a set of parents and their children ranging from age five to age fourteen, revealed results that surprised many of the participating parents: "Thirty-nine percent of parents who reported that their children did not know the storage location of household guns and twenty-two percent of parents who reported that their children had never handled a household gun were contradicted by their children's reports." Furthermore, the researchers concluded, "[P]arents who locked their guns away and discussed gun safety with their children were as likely to be contradicted as parents who did not take such safety measures." And as noted in Boodman's piece "In Harm's Way: Guns and Kids," "[F]ive-year-olds were just as likely to report [handling a gun in the home] as 14-year-olds."

So what can be done to prevent kids from encountering firearms? According to many gun-control proponents, Child Access Prevention (CAP) laws are the best option. As explained by the Brady Campaign to Prevent Gun Violence on its Web site www.bradycampaign.org, "Often referred to as 'Safe Storage' or 'gun owner responsibility' laws, [CAP laws] generally require adults to either store loaded guns in a place that is reasonably inaccessible to children, or use a device to lock the gun. If a child obtains an improperly stored, loaded gun, the adult owner is criminally liable."

The first state to pass such a law was Florida in 1989, and since then, the legislatures or courts in eighteen other states have established similar laws. Do such laws work? Some studies indicate they do. The 1997 study "State Gun Safe Storage Laws and Child Mortality Due to Firearms," published in the *Journal of the American Medical Association (JAMA)*, found this:

> Laws that make gun owners responsible for storing firearms in a manner that makes them inaccessible to children were in effect for at least I year in 12 states from 1990 through 1994. Among children younger than 15 years, unintentional shooting deaths were reduced by 23% (95% confidence interval, 6%–37%) during the years covered by these laws. This estimate was based on within-state comparisons adjusted for national trends in unintentional firearm-related mortality.

The study concluded, "State safe storage laws intended to make firearms less accessible to children appear to prevent unintentional shooting deaths among children younger than 15 years."

Gun-control opponents, however, argue that the study published in *JAMA* and embraced by the anti-gun lobby fails to address the fact that accidental firearm deaths among America's youth began to decline in the mid-1970s, not upon the introduction of CAP laws in 1989, and that deaths have decreased nationwide, not only in the states subject to the CAP laws.

## Criticism of CAP Laws and Alternatives to Reducing Gun-Related Accidents

Some critics of CAP laws claim that they interfere with people's rights to self-defense and privacy. They contend that home safety is the responsibility of the individual, not the state. The NRA, for instance, maintains that laws mandating trigger locks and safe-storage requirements are unnecessary. The group argues that "one-size-fits-all" storage requirements are counterproductive, since the circumstances and needs of gun owners vary greatly. In addition, the NRA points out that trigger locks can handicap a gun owner when a firearm is needed for personal protection, and that such devices are not a substitute for safe handling practices, since locks can fail. Furthermore, the pro-gun lobby attests that irresponsible people are unlikely to comply with CAP laws, and that enforcement of storage laws can lead to violations of civil liberties.

While opposed to CAP laws, gun advocates promote gun-safety education as an effective method of preventing gun violence among children. The most widely used program is the NRA's Eddie Eagle GunSafe Program, which since its start in 1988, has been presented in schools across the United States, in time spans ranging from one-day lessons to five-day programs. The program's description, as detailed on the NRA Web site www.nrahq.org, notes that it was developed by a team of "such qualified professionals as clinical psychologists, reading specialists, teachers, curriculum specialists, urban housing safety officials, and law enforcement personnel." When working with the children, Eddie Eagle does not present an opinion on whether guns are good or bad in general, and he never touches a firearm in the children's presence. He teaches the kids that they should never touch one, either. Children are instructed to immediately leave the area if they find a gun and to immediately notify an adult.

The NRA reports that the program is successful and points, for example, to a 2001 *Journal of Emergency Nursing Online* study that named Eddie Eagle the best of the gun-accident prevention programs reviewed in the study. The NRA also cites correspondence from parents who report that when their children have encountered guns, they have followed Eddie Eagle's instructions.

## Disagreement over Gun Safety

Some analysts and organizations outside the NRA are not convinced of the Eddie Eagle program's effectiveness. The *Washington Post* paraphrased Matthew Miller, coauthor of the earlier-discussed study on parents' misconceptions about their children's experience with guns in the home and associate director of the Harvard Injury Control Research Center: "Relying solely on strategies that seek to dampen the natural curiosity of a child, such as telling children guns are dangerous, or assuming that a child will be unfailingly obedient and never touch a weapon if he finds one, is ineffective at best." For the same article, Jon Vernick of the Center for Gun Policy and Research at Johns Hopkins Bloomberg School of Public Health said: "Teaching kids to be safe around guns doesn't work." The article continues, "Studies have found that children exposed to Eddie Eagle programs are no less likely to play with guns than children who don't take the class."

Instead, Vernick promotes the public-service campaign ASK, which stands for "Asking Saves Kids" and which encourages parents to ask relatives and the parents of their children's playmates about guns in those homes, even if the parents already have safe gun practices in their own homes. And as gun-control advocates avow, children often know and do more than their parents think. A gun well-hidden, they attest, is not the same as a gun locked and unloaded. Similarly, a key well-hidden is not the same as a key on the parent's person—and unavailable to the child—at all times. Naturally curious, children snoop, and they find what adults think they will not or cannot, as did the ten-year-old son of a New York City police officer in 2006: he died after accidentally shooting himself in the face with his father's revolver. He had found the gun hidden on a basement shelf while looking for a ball his mother had taken away from him. In contrast, a seven-year-old girl from Michigan saved her two younger brothers from harm when, upon finding a gun in the corner of a closet during a game of hide-and-seek, she commanded her siblings to "Stop! Don't Touch. Leave the Area. Tell an Adult," as she had been taught.

Although the debate continues concerning the best ways to stop gun violence among children and teens, it is clear that advocates on both sides of the controversy are passionate about their commitment to keeping children safe. Gun enthusiasts believe that education is the key to gun safety, while anti-gunners maintain that firearm-safety education is insufficient in preventing gun violence among young people.

# CHAPTER 1

# Can the States Prohibit Citizens from Keeping and Bearing Arms?

# Chapter Preface

## Case Overview: *Presser v. Illinois* (1886)

On September 27, 1879, Herman Presser, a U.S. and Illinois citizen, was indicted in Cook County, Illinois, under Article 11 of Illinois's military code. As the leader of Lehr und Wehr Verein—a group of German immigrants legally formed in 1875 "for the purpose of improving the mental and bodily condition of its members so as to qualify them for the duties of citizens of a republic"—Presser, on horseback and carrying a sword, had led 400 armed members of this group in a parade in the streets of Chicago. Although the rifles reportedly were not loaded, the group nonetheless acted in violation of Illinois law, which forbade "any body of men whatever, other than the regular organized volunteer militia of this state, and the troops of the United States, to associate themselves together as a military company or organization, or to drill or parade with arms in any city or town of this state, without the license of the governor thereof." Presser did not have said permission from Illinois's governor.

After the court denied the defense's motion to quash the indictment, Presser pled not guilty and waived his right to a jury trial. The court subsequently found him guilty and fined him $10. Presser's attorneys, Allan C. Story and Lyman Trumbull, appealed the decision to the Illinois Supreme Court, which affirmed the lower court's judgment. Ultimately, the U.S. Supreme Court agreed to hear the case, though it did not hand down its decision until more than six years after the initial indictment.

Presser's position in the U.S. Supreme Court was that the law under which he was indicted and convicted was itself void and unconstitutional because it contradicted his Second Amendment right to keep and bear arms. Indeed, the appeal of the *Presser* case seemed to have more to do with trying to set, or reverse, precedent than with concern over Herman Presser's individual case and minimal fine. The militia as described in the Constitution, Presser's attorneys argued, called for the entire male population to be a part of that militia, and Presser and his men were merely making sure that they were ready for such a responsibility.

The state of Illinois, on the other hand, argued that it had the right to organize its militias according to its own rules and regulations and that the right to keep and bear arms did not extend to Presser the right to assemble an armed, unsanctioned militia to publicly drill in violation of Illinois state law. The Court agreed, with Justice William Burnham Woods penning the decision.

The Supreme Court found that Illinois's law did not violate citizens' right to bear arms because the sections of law at issue in this case only forbade citizens from associating and parading, without license, as armed military entities, not from simply keeping and bearing arms generally. Furthermore, the Court found, in keeping with the precedent of *U.S. v. Cruikshank* (1876), that the Second Amendment, regardless, did not apply to the states: "the amendment is a limitation only upon the power of congress and the national government, and not upon the state." Still, the Court did also clarify that "all citizens capable of bearing arms constitute the reserved military force or reserve militia" and that the states cannot prohibit citizens from keeping and bearing arms generally, thus establishing some precedents for both sides of the gun-control argument.

> "[T]he sections [of the Military Code of Illinois] under consideration ... do not infringe the right of the people to keep and bear arms."

# The Court's Decision: States Can Control and Regulate Private Military Groups and Associations

## Justice William Burnham Woods

*Justice William Burnham Woods was a major general in the Union Army and former mayor of Newark, Ohio. He was elected to the House of Representatives of Ohio and served as speaker. In 1880 he was nominated to the Supreme Court by President Rutherford B. Hayes. He served six years on the bench until his death in 1887 at age sixty-two.*

*Justice William Burnham Woods wrote and delivered the Court's opinion in the case of* Presser v. Illinois *(1886), excerpted here. The plaintiff, Herman Presser, was found guilty of violating Illinois law when he paraded with a group of armed men without authorization. Presser claimed that the Military Code of Illinois violated his Second Amendment right to keep and bear arms. The Court ruled that the state legislatures have the power to regulate military groups with the exception of those protected by federal militia laws. The Court reaffirmed the precedent set forth in* United States v. Cruikshank *(1876) that the Second Amendment does not limit the power of state governments. Woods further explained that because all capable citizens comprise the fed-*

Justice William Burnham Woods, majority opinion, *Presser v. Illinois*, 1886.

*eral government's reserved military force, the states cannot restrict the rights of citizens to keep and bear arms because this action would conflict with the constitutional right of Congress to maintain a militia.*

The position of the plaintiff in error in this court was that the entire statute under which he was convicted was invalid and void because its enactment was the exercise of a power by the legislature of Illinois forbidden to the states by the constitution of the United States. The clauses of the constitution of the United States referred to in the assignments of error were as follows:

> Article 1, 8. The congress shall have power ... to raise and support armies; ... to provide for calling forth the militia to execute the laws of the Union, suppress insurrections, and repel invasions; to provide for organizing, arming, and disciplining the militia, and for governing such part of them as may be employed in the service of the United States, reserving to the states, respectively, the appointment of the officers, and the authority of training the militia, according to the discipline prescribed by congress; ... to make all laws which shall be necessary and proper, for carrying into execution the foregoing powers, etc.

> Article 1, 10. No state shall, without the consent of congress, keep troops ... in time of peace.

> Art. 2 of Amendments. A well regulated militia being necessary to the security of a free state, the right of the people to keep and bear arms shall not be infringed.

The plaintiff in error also contended that the enactment of the fifth and sixth sections of article 11 of the Military Code was forbidden by subdivision 3 of section 9 of article 1, which declares 'no bill of attainder or ex post facto law shall be passed,' and by article 14 of Amendments, which provides that 'no state shall make or enforce any law which shall abridge the privileges or immunities of citizens of the United States, nor shall any state deprive any person of life, liberty, or property without due process of law.'

The first contention of counsel for plaintiff in error is that the congress of the United States having, by virtue of the provisions of article 1 of section 8, above quoted, passed the act of May 8, 1792, entitled 'An act more effectually to provide for the national defense by establishing an uniform militia throughout the United States,' the act of February 28, 1795, 'to provide for calling forth the militia to execute the laws of the Union, suppress insurrections, and repel invasions,' and the act of July 22, 1861, 'to authorize the employment of volunteers to aid in enforcing the laws and protecting public property,' and other subsequent acts, now forming 'Title 16, The Militia,' of the Revised Statutes of the United States, the legislature of Illinois had no power to pass the act approved May 28, 1879, 'to provide for the organization of the state militia, entitled the "Military Code of Illinois,"' under the provisions of which (sections 5 and 6 of article 11) the plaintiff in error was indicted.

The argument in support of this contention is, that the power of organizing, arming, and disciplining the militia being confided by the constitution to congress, when it acts upon the subject, and passes a law to carry into effect the constitutional provision, such action excludes the power of legislation by the state on the same subject.

## The Military Code of Illinois

It is further argued that the whole scope and object of the Military Code of Illinois is in conflict with that of the law of congress. It is said that the object of the act of congress is to provide for organizing, arming, and disciplining all the able-bodied male citizens of the states, respectively, between certain ages, that they may be ready at all times to respond to the call of the nation to enforce its laws, suppress insurrection, and repel invasion, and thereby avoid the necessity for maintaining a large standing army, with which liberty can never be safe, and that, on the other hand, the effect if not object of the Illinois statute is to prevent such organizing, arming, and disciplining of the militia.

The plaintiff in error insists that the act of congress requires absolutely all able-bodied citizens of the state, between certain ages, to be enrolled in the militia; that the act of Illinois makes the enrollment dependent on the necessity for the use of troops to execute the laws and suppress insurrections, and then leaves it discretionary with the governor by proclamation to require such enrollment; that the act of congress requires the entire enrolled militia of the state, with a few exemptions made by it and which may be made by state laws, to be formed into companies, battalions, regiments, brigades, and divisions; that every man shall be armed and supplied with ammunition; provides a system of discipline and field exercises for companies, regiments, etc., and subjects the entire militia of the state to the call of the president to enforce the laws, suppress insurrection, or repel invasion, and provides for the punishment of the militia officers and men who refuse obedience to his orders. On the other hand, it is said that the state law makes it unlawful for any of its able-bodied citizens, except 8,000, called the 'Illinois National Guard,' to associate themselves together as a military company, or to drill or parade with arms without the license of the governor, and declares that no military company shall leave the state with arms and equipments without his consent; that even the 8,000 men styled the 'Illinois National Guard' are not enrolled or organized as required by the act of congress, nor are they subject to the call of the president, but they constitute a military force sworn to serve in the military service of the state, to obey the orders of the governor, and not to leave the state without his consent; and that, if the state act is valid, the national act providing for organizing, arming, and disciplining the militia is of no force in the state of Illinois, for the Illinois act, so far from being in harmony with the act of congress, is an insurmountable obstacle to its execution. We have not found it necessary to consider or decide the question thus raised as to the validity of the entire Military Code of Illinois, for, in our opinion, the sections under which the plaintiff in error was convicted may be valid, even if the other sections of the act were invalid. For it is a settled rule 'that statutes that are constitutional in part only will be upheld so far as they are not in conflict with the constitution, provided the allowed and prohibited parts are separable.' . . .

## The Illinois State Law Does Not Violate the Right to Bear Arms

We are next to inquire whether the fifth and sixth sections of article 11 of the Military Code are in violation of the other provisions of the constitution of the United States relied on by the plaintiff in error. The first of these is the second amendment, which declares: 'A well regulated militia being necessary to the security of a free state, the right of the people to keep and bear arms shall not be infringed.'

We think it clear that the sections under consideration, which only forbid bodies of men to associate together as military organizations, or to drill or parade with arms in cities and towns unless authorized by law, do not infringe the right of the people to keep and bear arms. But a conclusive answer to the contention that this amendment prohibits the legislation in question lies in the fact that the amendment is a limitation only upon the power of congress and the national government, and not upon that of the state. It was so held by this court in the case of *U.S. v. Cruikshank*, in which the chief justice, in delivering the judgment of the court, said that the right of the people to keep and bear arms 'is not a right granted by the constitution. Neither is it in any manner dependent upon that instrument for its existence. The second amendment declares that it shall not be infringed, but this, as has been seen, means no more than that it shall not be infringed by congress. This is one of the amendments that has no other effect than to restrict the powers of the national government, leaving the people to look for their protection against any violation by their fellow-citizens of the rights it recognizes to what is called in *City of New York v. Miln*, the 'powers which relate to merely municipal legislation, or what was perhaps more properly called internal police,' 'not surrendered or restrained' by the constitution of the United States.'

It is undoubtedly true that all citizens capable of bearing arms constitute the reserved military force or reserve militia of the United States as well as of the states, and, in view of this prerogative of the general government, as well as of its general powers, the states cannot, even laying the constitutional provision in question out of view, prohibit the people from keeping and bearing arms, so as to deprive the United States of their rightful resource for maintaining the public security, and disable the people from performing their duty to the general government. But, as already stated, we think it clear that the sections under consideration do not have this effect.

*"Courts thus far have been reluctant to invalidate gun control laws under any constitutional provision. . . . State and local governments are not bound by the Second Amendment."*

# Limits on the Power of States to Regulate Firearms

*Regina McClendon*

*Regina McClendon wrote the following article while a law student at University of California, Hastings College of the Law. Five years later, in 1999, McClendon joined the California law firm of Severson & Werson, where she practices in the area of financial services litigation. She serves on the editorial board of advisers of the* Consumer Financial Services Law Report *and is editor in chief of her firm's quarterly* Consumer Law Report.

*In this article, Regina McClendon uses debate in California over state gun-control legislation at the time the article was written as a starting point for a discussion of California's and other states' rights to regulate firearms. She includes analysis of the argument that state-imposed gun-control legislation is prohibited by the federal Second Amendment, exploring the varying interpretations of the right to bear arms. McClendon also addresses the debate over the interpretation of the California constitution, which gives the individual the right to own firearms but does not specifically address the right to bear those arms. She concludes that the Second Amendment prohibits only the federal*

Regina McClendon, "Limits on the Power of States to Regulate Firearms," Public Law Research Institute, Hastings College of Law, Fall, 1994. Copyright © 1994, University of California, Hastings College of the Law. Reproduced by permission.

*government's interference with the right to bear arms and does not apply to state and local governments, which are therefore not barred from passing gun-control legislation. In the specific case of California, she determines, the state constitution does not guarantee the right to bear arms.*

Although state gun control legislation is proposed as one method of controlling the spread of firearms in California, there are many objections raised. This paper explores the validity of these objections, focusing [on] federal and state constitutional rights and prohibitions. (A related paper analyzes constitutional rights of the individual and state that would prevent the federal government from passing gun control legislation.)

First, the federal Constitution's prohibition on interfering with the "right to bear arms" is examined, and alternative constructions are analyzed to see whether this is considered a right conferred on individuals or on the state. Regardless of the construction used, the Second Amendment prohibition has no effect on state legislatures wishing to formulate gun control measures.

A second argument used to prevent the California legislature from passing gun control legislation is that the California Constitution also confers an individual right of the individual to own guns. The California Constitution contains nothing explicit, however, on the right to bear arms. Finally, some common constitutional methods of challenging state gun control legislation are discussed, though virtually none of these have been successful.

## The Scope of the Second Amendment: Individual Right or State Right?

The question of whether the Second Amendment confers an individual right to bear arms or merely prohibits the federal government from interfering with the state militia has not been clearly decided by the Supreme Court. The individual right approach treats the Second Amendment as a right of individual citizens which cannot be restricted by the federal government. The more popular interpretation, the state's right approach, characterizes the Second Amendment as a right granted to the states that cannot be infringed by the federal government. Though the Supreme Court has remained silent on the scope of the Second Amendment, both of these academic interpretations of the right to bear arms have been discussed by at least one federal appeals court.

*The Individual Right Approach* Under the individual right interpretation, the federal government may not completely prohibit individual gun ownership. The question of whether a state may prohibit gun ownership is less clear; the answer depends on whether the Second Amendment has been applied to the states through the doctrine of selective incorporation.

*The Doctrine of Selective Incorporation.* The Bill of Rights only protects citizens against action by the federal government. However, through the doctrine of selective incorporation, the Supreme Court has held that the Due Process Clause of the Fourteenth Amendment may limit action by state and local governments as well. Nevertheless, the Supreme Court rejects the notion that the Fourteenth Amendment incorporates the entire Bill of Rights. Instead, the Court has decided on a case by case basis which rights are so "fundamental" as to be brought into the Fourteenth Amendment and to bind state and local governments. However, ambiguity remains. Some provisions of the Bill of Rights have still not been considered by the Supreme Court since it began applying the incorporation doctrine.

The Second Amendment is not among those rights incorporated into the Fourteenth Amendment, In *United States v. Cruikshank* [1876] the Supreme Court held that "the second amendment . . . means no more than that it shall not be infringed by Congress." Subsequently, in *Presser v. Illinois* [1886], the Court rejected a claim that the Second Amendment could invalidate a state law. In that case, the Court upheld an Illinois statute which made it unlawful for a group other than the state militia or federal troops to drill or parade with arms in public without permission from the governor. The defendant argued that this law violated the Second Amendment guarantee of the right to bear arms. Relying on *Cruikshank*, the Court disagreed, reasoning that "the amendment is a limitation only upon the power of Congress and the National government, and not upon that of the states."

*The Validity of Nonincorporation.* Because the Second Amendment has never been explicitly addressed in formal incorporation analysis, the conclusion that the amendment only applies to actions by the federal government has been questioned. The decisions in *Cruikshank* and *Presser* came several years before any provisions of the Bill of Rights were incorporated, thus one cannot be sure that the justices in the Second Amendment cases considered the possibility of incorporation.

The first incorporation decision occurred in 1897, eleven years after *Presser* and twenty-two years after *Cruikshank*. Today, only three provisions of the Bill of Rights, including the Second, Fifth and Seventh Amendments, remain unincorporated. The almost total incorporation of the Bill of Rights lends support to the theory that incorporation of the Second Amendment is inevitable. However, more than one hundred years have passed since *Cruikshank* and *Presser* were decided, during which time the Supreme Court has been content to let those decisions stand.

The Supreme Court's reluctance to revisit the Second Amendment incorporation question is most notable in its refusal to hear an appeal of a case in which the Seventh Circuit upheld a local government's ban on possession of handguns within its borders. The appeals court, citing *Presser*, based its decision on the nonapplicability of the Second Amendment to state and local governments.

Likewise, the Ninth Circuit has followed *Cruikshank* and *Presser* in upholding California's Roberti-Roos Assault Weapons Control Act of 1989 (AWCA). The plaintiffs attempted to have the AWCA declared unconstitutional on several grounds, including arguing that the law violates the Second Amendment right to bear arms. The court rejected this argument, holding that the Second Amendment only binds the federal government. This case was never appealed to the Supreme Court.

More than a century after they were decided, *Cruikshank* and *Presser* remain good law. Thus, the right to bear arms granted by the Constitution, if analyzed as an individual right, only limits the federal government's attempts to restrict firearms. State and local governments are not bound by the Second Amendment.

*The State's Right Approach* The alternate interpretation of the Second Amendment, the state's right approach, has received more support in Supreme Court opinions than has the individual right theory. Under this analysis, the right to bear arms has no application to state legislation, and means only that the federal government may impose any firearm restriction so long as it does not impede a state's militia.

In *United States v. Miller*, the Supreme Court, noting that the purpose of the Second Amendment was to ensure an effective militia, upheld a federal law banning the transport in interstate commerce and subsequent ownership of sawed off shotguns. The Court found that such weapons may be prohibited because they bear no reasonable relationship to a well regulated state militia. Moreover, the Supreme Court recently cited *Miller* in support of its conclusion that Congress may restrict firearm possession by felons because such a law does not impair a state's right to preserve its militia.

These decisions suggest that the Court favors a Second Amendment test that determines whether the prohibited weapon bears a reasonable relationship to the state militia.

Such a test presumes that the Second Amendment is a right granted to states, not to individuals. In practice, courts allow the federal government broad power to restrict firearms: since the *Miller* decision in 1939, "no federal court has found any individual's possession of a military weapon to be reasonably related to a well regulated militia."

*Second Amendment Conclusion* Under the state's right analysis, the Second Amendment only restricts federal government action and imposes no barrier to state or local governments.

Likewise, if an individual right analysis is used, only the federal government is bound by the Second Amendment. State and local governments are not restricted as long as the Second Amendment remains unincorporated into the Fourteenth Amendment.

## The California Constitution

The California Constitution does not contain a provision guaranteeing the right to bear arms. Furthermore, because the Second Amendment does not apply to state legislation, California state laws are not subject to U.S. constitutional attacks based on the right to bear arms. The California Supreme Court notes that the claim that a weapons regulation "violates the Second Amendment has been rejected by every court which has ruled on the question." The court also states that "[i]t is long since settled in this state that regulation of firearms is a proper police function." Therefore, absent a state constitutional amendment, California firearms restrictions are not limited by the right to bear arms.

## Other Arguments Against State Gun Control Legislation

Gun control legislation has been challenged on a wide variety of bases with virtually no success. Some of the more common methods for challenging weapons regulations are discussed below. However, most challenges are fact-specific to their particular case. Therefore, this list is merely illustrative of some possible arguments.

*Fifth Amendment of the U.S. Constitution* The Fifth Amendment privilege against self-incrimination was used to invalidate a portion of the National Firearms Act of 1934. The privilege against self-incrimination permits persons to refuse to give inculpatory testimony. The Act contained a gun registration requirement that was directed primarily at persons who had obtained weapons illegally. The Supreme Court found that requiring such persons to register their weapons forced them to incriminate themselves for these other criminal acts.

However, the self-incrimination argument ultimately failed. After Congress rewrote the offending provision by only requiring lawful possessors of firearms to register, the Supreme Court ruled that the Act no longer violates the privilege against self-incrimination.

*Ninth Amendment of the U.S. Constitution* Parties have argued that the right to possess firearms for the purpose of self-defense, if not explicitly listed in the Bill of Rights, is a right contained in the Ninth Amendment. The Ninth Amendment states that "[t]he enumeration in the Constitution of certain rights shall not be construed to deny or disparage others retained by the people." The Seventh Circuit rejected this argument, finding no Supreme Court precedent to support the theory that the Ninth Amendment protects any specific right. In fact, the Ninth Amendment has not been used to define the rights of individuals or to invalidate state or federal laws.

*Preemption* The argument that state gun control legislation is preempted by federal law has not been accepted. The supremacy clause of the Constitution requires that federal law override conflicting state law. The Ninth Circuit explains that preemption generally occurs when Congress has explicitly or implicitly intended to supersede state law. The court also notes that "Congress expressly disavowed any intent to occupy the field of gun control in the Gun Control Act of 1968." In fact, the purpose of the Act was to assist the states in regulating firearms. Furthermore, the Act mandates compliance with state and local gun control laws. Thus, it cannot be argued that Congress intended to supersede state legislation.

## The Current Climate

Courts thus far have been reluctant to invalidate gun control laws under any constitutional provision, particularly the Second Amendment. Under either the individual right analysis or the state's right analysis the conclusion is the same: state and local governments are not bound by the Second Amendment. Furthermore, the California Constitution does not contain a provision guaranteeing the right to bear arms. Finally, other constitutional arguments for invalidating state legislation generally have been unsuccessful or, if successful, state constitutional defects have been corrected by Congress.

*"The Second Amendment right of the people to keep and bear arms . . . should be considered as protected from state infringement by the Fourteenth Amendment."*

# The Second Amendment Does Not Apply to the States

*Stephen P. Halbrook*

*Stephen P. Halbrook has been practicing civil litigation and criminal defense since receiving his Juris Doctor from Georgetown University Law Center in 1978. With a PhD in philosophy, he has also taught at several universities. Among his published books are* Firearms Law Deskbook: Federal and State Criminal Practice *(2005);* Freedmen, the Fourteenth Amendment, and the Right to Bear Arms, 1866–1876 *(1998); and* Target Switzerland: Swiss Armed Neutrality in World War II *(1998).*

*In his examination of* Presser v. Illinois *and the case's historical contexts and future implications, Stephen P. Halbrook explores the U.S. Supreme Court's decision and the reasons behind it. He posits that the Supreme Court, for various reasons, failed to consider the Due Process Clause of the Fourteenth Amendment when deciding whether the Second Amendment applied to the states. He concludes that the* Presser *opinion "belongs to a bygone era" and that the Second Amendment should indeed apply to the states.*

Stephen P. Halbrook, "The Right of Workers to Assemble and to Bear Arms: *Presser v. Illinois,* One of the Last Holdouts Against Application of the Bill of Rights to the States," *University of Detroit Mercy Law Review,* vol. 76, no. 4, Summer 1999, pp. 943–89. Copyright © 1999 University of Detroit Mercy Law Review. Reproduced by permission.

Is the right of workers—like that of members of other classes—to assemble and to bear arms protected by the United States Constitution from violation by the States? If this question sounds like it was posed during the "labor struggles" of the second half of the nineteenth century, it is because it was. During that epoch, the Supreme Court held that the Bill of Rights guarantees did not limit state action and read the Fourteenth Amendment narrowly. This era is epitomized by *Presser v. Illinois* [1886] which held, *inter alia*, that an armed march in a city went far beyond the rights to assemble and to keep and bear arms and that the due process clause of the Fourteenth Amendment was not relevant to such issues.

## *Presser* Is Role in Subsequent Rulings

From the Great Strike of 1873 to 1887, when the Supreme Court sealed the fate of the defendants who were condemned to death for the Haymarket Riot, conflict between the industrialists and their workers in Chicago, Illinois, gave rise to divisive legal rulings, which continue to this day. While the holding in *Presser* that the right to assembly is not protected from state violation passed by the wayside over a half century ago, its statement that the right to bear arms is not shielded from state infringement continues to be cited currently to uphold prohibitions on firearms possession. Indeed, the enduring legacy of *Presser* is its citation for the proposition that the Second Amendment does not apply to the states.

Thus in a 1998 decision, the Sixth Circuit invalidated a local "assault weapon" ban as unconstitutionally vague and violative of equal protection clause of the Fourteenth Amendment. It added, *sua sponte* and in dictum, that the law was not an invalid infringement of the right to keep and bear arms, because *Presser* held that the Second Amendment did not apply to the states. In 1992, the Ninth Circuit upheld America's first state "assault weapon" ban on that basis.

Ironically, just as *Presser* arose out of Chicago, America's first handgun ban was passed in Morton Grove, a Chicago suburb, and upheld by the Seventh Circuit in 1983, which relied on *Presser*.

Yet, did *Presser* actually consider whether the Fourteenth Amendment's due process clause protected the right to keep and bear arms from state infringement? Is *Presser* a relic of a distant era of labor conflict? Does it endure, notwithstanding the Supreme Court's jurisprudence in the twentieth century, which incorporated nearly every one of the Bill of Rights' guarantees into the Fourteenth Amendment?

## Labor Conflicts and the Abolition of Slavery

A return to that lost milieu of labor conflict illustrates how both statutory enactments and case law reflect power structures in societies—for example, how the Illinois legislature acted to weed workers out of the state militia in order to use that force to break strikes and how the Illinois and United States Supreme Courts upheld such actions. Included in this milieu is a Chicago judge's opinion, which remains one of the most remarkable decisions ever rendered on the right to bear arms and which invalidated the restrictive militia law of the state. This intrepid judge was labeled a tool of foreign "communists." An analysis of the *Presser* epoch offers a significant contribution to the history of labor conflict and its legal consequences, and depicts the influence of popular views on the rendering of judicial decisions.

Only when slavery was abolished in 1865 and the newly freed slaves demanded all the rights of citizenship did the right to assemble and the right to bear arms become controversial. In 1868, the Fourteenth Amendment to the Constitution was ratified primarily to protect these rights of the newly freed slaves under the Bill of Rights from violation by the States, when the South sought to reenact the slave codes. However, at the end of the Reconstruction in 1876, the United

States Supreme Court held that the First and Second Amendments did not protect the rights of freed slaves to assemble and to bear arms from private violators, such as members of the Ku Klux Klan.

By that time, an aspiring labor movement, which included many recent immigrants, was beginning to flourish, demanding better working conditions and frightening the members of the economic elite. Working class meetings and demonstrations were increasingly subjected to violent dispersal by police forces and troops. The time had come, the forces of "order" believed, to curtail labor agitation and to restrict public assemblies and the bearing of arms to loyal Americans of the middle and upper classes.

It was against this backdrop that German-American workers in Chicago, Illinois, in the 1870s and the 1880s brought several test cases in the courts, concerning the rights to assemble and bear arms. These cases arose in the context of the perceived use of the police and the newly created "National Guard" (actually a State armed force) by those in power against industrial workers who were intent on bettering their working conditions. Those who initiated the litigation through protest acts behaved in a nonviolent manner to secure what they perceived to be their constitutional rights. Their goal was the official recognition of their rights by the courts of justice.

Relying on traditional American concepts of individual rights as well as similar liberal influences from the Revolution of 1848 in Germany, they initially won a historic legal victory. This victory would be rolled back by the higher courts in other cases. Defeat would turn to tragedy as a result of the Haymarket riot of 1886, in which people died—both at the scene and later on the gallows—and, with them, a bit of the Bill of Rights. Responding to what many perceived as a threat to the social order, the members of the United States Supreme Court approved of what has been characterized as the disarming of unions and the reduction of jury autonomy. . . .

## *Presser v. Illinois* in the United States Supreme Court

The case of *Presser v. Illinois* was finally argued in the U.S. Supreme Court in November 1885. Presser was represented by Allan C. Story and Lyman Trumbull, whose brief in the *Dunne* [*v. People of the State of Illinois* (1879)] case was also submitted. Presser's brief did not raise the issue of whether the Fourteenth Amendment protects the individual's right to keep and bear arms. Instead, Presser argued that the militia should consist of the entire male populace. Presser queried:

> What *security against usurpation*, would be found in a volunteer (Governor's) guard, of limited strength, and the balance of the people practically disarmed, and their *organization and arming, stamped as a criminal offense*, except it be done with the consent, of the very man, against those usurpation of powers, their organization and arming may, perhaps be directed, and lawfully so[?]

Presser argued that the Second Amendment right of the people to bear arms was a right "to be exercised in their collective, not less than in their individual capacity." Presser continued:

> "To bear arms", then, in the constitutional sense, means to bear the weapons of civilized warfare, and to become instructed in their use. But this is drilling, officering, organizing; therefore, these are claimed to be part and parcel, of the same impregnable right, and placed by the supreme law of the land, beyond the reach of infringement by the provisions of any military code or, the precarious will, and license of whoever may happen to be Governor.

Illinois Attorney General George Hunt's brief in *Presser* argued that the States had ample power to organize their militias as they saw fit. The State's power to organize a militia did not derive from the U.S. Constitution, but existed before its adoption, and was not prohibited by it. Furthermore, Hunt maintained that "the right to keep and bear arms by no means includes the right to assemble and publicly parade in the manner forbidden by the law under which the conviction in this case was had."

## The U.S. Supreme Court Affirms Presser's Conviction

On January 4, 1886, seven years after Presser's march, the U.S. Supreme Court affirmed his conviction. The *Presser* opinion was written by Justice William Woods. A decade earlier, as a circuit judge during the Reconstruction period, Woods had presided over federal criminal prosecutions against members of the Ku Klux Klan for violating the rights of blacks to assemble and to bear arms. Circuit Judge Woods had opined that both the federal government and the States were prohibited from abridging fights guaranteed by the Bill of Rights. In one famous case, Judge Woods instructed the jury that "every citizen of the United States has the right to bear arms," which is "secured by the Constitution." His instruction in that case that the rights to assemble and to bear arms were federally-protected from *private* conspiracy would be rejected by the Supreme Court in *United States v. Cruikshank* [1876].

Ten years later in *Presser*, Justice Woods concluded that the Second Amendment right of individuals to have arms did not preclude a State law requiring a license from the governor for an armed march by a military unit in a city. He stated:

> The sections under consideration, which only forbid bodies of men to associate together as military organizations, or to drill or parade with arms in cities and towns unless authorized by law, do not infringe the right of the people to keep and bear arms. But a conclusive answer to the contention that this amendment prohibits the legislation in question lies in the fact that the amendment is a limitation only upon the power of Congress and the National government, and not upon that of the state.

Thus, the Court held that the armed paraders exceeded the individual right of keeping and bearing of arms, adding that the Second Amendment does not apply directly to the States. Among the authorities cited for the latter proposition was an ante-bellum North Carolina opinion upholding a law prohibiting free blacks from carrying firearms on the basis that the free people of color cannot be considered as citizens and that the states are not mentioned in the Second Amendment, which "is therefore only restrictive of the powers of the Federal Government." The Court's reliance on this and other ante-bellum cases reinforces the fact that the Court did not consider whether the Fourteenth Amendment, adopted after the Civil War, protected Bill of Rights guarantees.

## States Cannot Deprive the Federal Government of a Militia

*Presser* did, however, recognize that the States may not infringe on the right to keep and bear arms in a manner that would deprive the federal government of the militia:

> All citizens capable of bearing arms constitute the reserved military force or reserve militia of the United States as well as of the states, and, in view of this prerogative of the general government ... the states cannot, even laying the constitutional provision in question out of view, prohibit the people from keeping and bearing arms, so as to deprive the United States of their rightful resource for maintaining the public security, and disable the people from performing their duty to the general government. But ... the sections under consideration do not have this effect.

## Bill of Rights Guarantees

Similarly, the Court rejected a First Amendment right of assembly argument applicable to Presser's band, because "the right voluntarily to associate together as a military company or organization, or to drill or parade with arms, ... is not an attribute of national citizenship." The states "have the power to regulate or prohibit associations and meetings of the people, except in the case of peaceable assemblies to perform the duties or exercises the privileges of citizens of the United States. . . ." After narrowly construing the right to assemble, the Court dramatically proclaimed: "To deny the power would be to deny the right of the State to disperse assemblages organized for sedition and treason, and the right to suppress armed mobs bent on riot and rapine." While the Court may have envisioned foreign-born, armed proletarians rioting in the streets, such facts were not before the Court. Conversely, the incident before the Court involved a peaceable march, where Presser intentionally got himself arrested, probably with the cooperation of local authorities, in order to test the law's validity.

Next, the Court summarily rejected Presser's argument that the law deprived him of life, liberty, or property without due process of law, because it was "so clearly untenable as to require no discussion." It is noteworthy, however, that beginning in 1897 and continuing throughout the twentieth century, the Court selectively incorporated most of the Bill of Rights guarantees into the due process clause of the Fourteenth Amendment. As indicated [earlier in this article], it never occurred to the *Presser* Court to consider whether the First and Second Amendments were protected by the Fourteenth Amendment's due process clause. The Court could have done so and still upheld the law in question.

Presser also argued that by providing for a select militia instead of the militia of all able-bodied males provided by federal law, the Illinois law was inconsistent with and preempted by the federal law.

The Court avoided deciding this argument by ruling that the provision under which Presser was convicted was severable from the militia provision.

## Analysis of the *Presser* Decision

Doctrine aside, the legal realist might conclude that *Presser* reflected the fear of the established interests toward the perceived challenges of foreigners and the laboring class. Similarly, in the preceding decade, in the face of the rising aspirations of the freedmen in the South, the Court seemed to read the Reconstruction Amendments narrowly.

Presser's attorney, Alan C. Story, was less than candid when he commented that the Court did not answer the question at stake, but "merely said that this particular case would not raise the question as to the right of the State to organize and keep a separate militia", which meant that the Lehr und Wehr Verein would have to obtain a permit from the Governor to march.

The *Central Law Journal*, whose contributors have included Supreme Court justices and distinguished scholars, reviewed the *Presser* decision and concluded:

> It will no doubt be news to most people, not members of the legal profession, and to many who are, that the Constitution of the United States does not secure to the citizens of the United States the right to "keep and bear arms." Such, however, is manifestly the effect of the ruling under consideration, the clause in the Second Amendment on that subject, the court regards as a limitation upon the powers of Congress, prohibiting that body and the general government from infringing that right. Whatever privileges therefore connected with bearing arms may be desired by any citizen, he must look for to his State, not to the United States.

## The Role of the Second and Fourteenth Amendments

In the twentieth century, the Supreme Court has held that most Bill of Rights guarantees [are] protected from State violation by the Fourteenth Amendment. The Court has remained silent on whether the right to bear arms is protected from state infringement by the Fourteenth Amendment.

What has been the legacy of *Presser* in the Supreme Court? *Presser* has been typically cited with other precedents for the proposition that the privileges-and-immunities clause of the Fourteenth Amendment does not protect Bill of Rights guarantees. It has been cited twice regarding the nature of the militia. Every relevant citation of *Presser* in a Supreme Court opinion was in the context of holding that *other* Bill of Rights guarantee[s], not including the Second Amendment, were inapplicable to the states.

All of the pertinent Supreme Court cases citing *Presser* held either that the Bill of Rights did not apply directly to the states or that the privileges-and-immunities clause of the Fourteenth Amendment did not incorporate the Bill of Rights. After this era of stingy interpretation of the Fourteenth Amendment had passed, the Supreme Court has incorporated most Bill of Rights guarantees under the due process clause of the Fourteenth Amendment. Because it failed to consider whether the Fourteenth Amendment's due process clause protects the Second Amendment, *Presser* has been obsolete for a century.

## Contemporary Views of the *Presser* Decision

Moreover, *Presser* has not been good company. It was cited with *Plessy v. Ferguson* [1896], which embraced the "separate-but-equal" doctrine of school segregation, for a narrow interpretation of the privileges and immunities protected from state action by the Fourteenth Amendment. *Presser* was also cited in one of the Court's worst decisions denigrating speech under the First Amendment. While the Supreme Court has not relied on *Presser* in recent times, *Presser* has been cited by various federal appellate courts to uphold local and state bans on handguns and on "assault weapons" (mostly rifles).

Apparently, these courts ignored the Supreme Court's last word on the subject, which was a 1894 ruling that its precedents established that the Bill of Rights did not apply to the states directly, and refusing to consider whether Bill of Rights guarantees (in that case, the Second and Fourth Amendments) applied to the states, because the issue was not raised in the courts below.

In concluding an analysis of the Supreme Court decisions in *Presser, Spies* [*v. United States* (1943)], and *Debs,* [*v. United States* (1919)] Professor L.H. LaRue stressed class conflict as the reality behind the legalisms:

> In that case [*Presser*], the Supreme Court endorsed the changes that were underway in other courts in which the right to bear arms was being limited. During these same years, the power of the jury to make final resolutions of a controversy was eliminated. Furthermore, freedom of speech was also sharply restricted. These changes go together if they are viewed in their historical context. The nineteenth century was a time of change. Different classes gained and lost unequally, which led to social unrest. Judges responded to these events by attempting to impose order. In this historical context the disarming of unions, the reduction of jury autonomy, the expansion of the injunction, and the restriction of radical speech form a coherent pattern. . . . The judges changed law in an attempt to deal with events thought to be serious threats to the social order in which they had a stake and to which they pledged loyalty.

Xenophobia, fear of the lower classes, and the desire to preserve the existing politico-economic order could well have been underlying premises for formal-sounding judicial decisions which gave the appearance of reliance on logic and precedent. However, such prejudices rarely invaded the decorum of a judicial decision. The decisions concerning the Lehr und Wehr Verein profoundly exemplify how the social milieu can influence—and limit—the contours of civil and constitutional rights as interpreted by the courts.

From the point of view of constitutional interpretation, *Presser* belongs to a bygone era of the nineteenth century, where the Supreme Court rejected the application of the Bill of Rights to the states without considering whether the Fourteenth Amendment, particularly its due process clause, made the Bill of Rights applicable to the states. In the twentieth century, however, almost all of the Bill of Rights' guarantees have been held applicable to the states. The structure of the amended Constitution and the logic of incorporation suggest that the Second Amendment right of the people to keep and bear arms, whatever its limits, should be considered as protected from state infringement by the Fourteenth Amendment.

*"Nothing in* Presser *says that the Second Amendment is not an individual right."*

# Anti-Gun Lobbyists Take the Supreme Court's Decision Out of Context

## Dave Kopel

*Dave Kopel, research director of the Independence Institute, holds a JD from the University of Michigan Law School and is a former assistant attorney general of Colorado. He is a regular contributor to* Liberty *magazine,* Rocky Mountain News, *and* National Review.

*Dave Kopel argues in the following article that "anti-gun lobbies" distort the meaning of* Presser v. Illinois *by treating it as a ruling that denied citizens' right to arms entirely, rather than as a ruling that upheld one specific type of gun control. In addition to upholding one gun-control law, Kopel writes, the Court also clarified limitations on states' gun-control laws and acknowledged gun ownership as a constitutional right under the Second Amendment.*

If you read the literature from the anti-gun lobbies you will be informed that the United States Supreme Court has "repeatedly" ruled that the Second Amendment is not an individual right. In this column, we'll look at the Supreme Court's most important gun case from the 19th century. This case is frequently cited by the anti-gun lobbies, but they cite the case for ideas which never appear in the case.

The case is *Presser v. Illinois* [1886]. The issue in *Presser* had nothing to do with whether the Second Amendment protected an individual right, but rather with the constitutionality of a particular gun control; a ban on parading a privately-formed, armed group down public streets.

## Historical Context for *Presser*

The late 19th century was a period in which state governments resorted to increasingly violent means to suppress organized labor. Unsurprisingly, many labor groups formed self-defense organizations. National Guard units and other state para-military forces (and occasionally the U.S. Army) were used to suppress strikes. Most workers' organizations were not interested in overthrowing the government, but only in protecting their right to choose to bargain collectively for decent working conditions and fair wages.

One prong of the governmental effort to suppress organized labor was a ban on armed parades in public; Illinois was one of the states that enacted such a ban, making it a crime for "bodies of men to associate together as military organizations, or to drill or parade with arms in cities and towns unless authorized by law. . ."

In response, a labor organization composed of German immigrants, Lehr und Wehr Verein, staged a parade in which they carried unloaded rifles. A prosecution ensued, and the case eventually got to the Supreme Court.

## The Supreme Court Decision

The Court had no difficulty upholding the law. First, the Court said that Illinois's legislation "does not infringe the right of the people to keep and bear arms." Explained the Court, "The exercise of this power by the States is necessary to the public peace, safety and good order. To deny the power would be to deny the right of the State to disperse assemblages organized for sedition and treason, and the right to suppress armed mobs bent on riot and rapine."

But the dispositive issue, according to the Court, was that, as the Court had ruled in previous cases, the entire Bill of Rights, including the Second Amendment, "is a limitation only upon the power of Congress and the National Government, and not upon that of the States."

In other words, the Bill of Rights only protected citizens against federal laws, not against state laws. (This doctrine was abandoned in the 20th century, but that's another story.)

## Current Implications

Now *Presser* is a good case for gun control advocates. The case upholds one particular kind of gun control, and could, arguably at least, be used as a foundation for bans on other collective exercises of the right to keep and bear arms. In addition, the case removes the Second Amendment as a barrier to state or local gun control.

It's questionable today whether *Presser* is good law, in light of various 20th-century cases, but *Presser* has never formally been over-ruled.

Yet the anti-gun lobbies, which could use *Presser* as a basis for gun-control, instead represent *Presser* as supposedly supporting the idea that there is no right to arms at all.

Of course, nothing in *Presser* says that the Second Amendment is not an individual right. In fact, one part of the *Presser* opinion erects a new limitation on gun prohibition.

## Limits on State Gun Laws

While *Presser* said that the Second Amendment does not protect gun owners against state laws, the *Presser* Court explained that a different section of the Constitution does limit state gun laws.

Article One, Section Eight of the Constitution grants Congress limited powers over the militia. (To call forth the militia in certain circumstances, and regulate militia training.) *In dicta* (a non-binding expression of opinion, not necessary to decide the case at bar), the Court noted that even if there were no Second Amendment, the states could not disarm their citizens, because such disarmaments would deprive Congress of its Article I power to regulate militia training and to call forth the militia:

> It is undoubtedly true that all citizens capable of bearing arms constitute the reserve military force or reserve militia of the United States; and, in view of this prerogative of the General Government, as well as of its general powers, the States cannot, even laying the constitutional provision in question [the Second Amendment] out of view, prohibit the people from keeping and bearing arms, so as to deprive the United States of their rightful resource for maintaining the public security, and disable the people from performing their duty to the general government. But, as already stated, we think it clear that the sections under consideration do not have this effect.

Thus, the Court states that the states may not "prohibit the people from keeping and bearing arms." Further, the militia is not a select, uniformed force, instead, the militia consists of "all citizens capable of bearing arms."

Thus, when the anti-gun lobbies claim that *Presser* not only supports gun control (which it does) but also says that there is no Constitutional barrier to gun prohibition, the lobbyists are wildly off-base.

## The Court's Acknowlegment of the Right to Gun Ownership

*Presser* is consistent with other Supreme Court cases on gun control. . . . While acknowledging that gun ownership is a Constitutional right, the Court upholds the particular gun control in question. Taking these cases at face value ought to be sufficient for groups which merely favor moderate gun controls. That gun control groups work so hard to take *Presser* and other cases out of context, and to invent claims that these cases mean there is no right to bear arms at all, shows a lot about the basic beliefs of the anti-gun groups. Rather than respecting gun ownership as a legitimate right subject to moderate controls, the anti-gun groups seek to destroy all Constitutional protection for gun ownership, leaving the government free to treat gun ownership as a severely regulated privilege with harsh restrictions (as the anti-gun lobby pragmatists would prefer) or to ban guns entirely (as the lobbies' more idealistic members would prefer).

> *"This case is about a body of men try-*
> *ing to make themselves ready to con-*
> *tribute to the security of a free State*
> *[and] a state which forbade them from*
> *doing so."*

# The Supreme Court's Attempt to Nullify the Second Amendment

## Bob Butler

*Bob Butler studied electronics engineering at Northeastern University.*

*In explaining his take on the case of* Presser v. Illinois, *Bob Butler briefly provides personal and cultural background information about Presser himself and establishes his reasons for finding that Presser and his comrades were acting according to the intent of the U.S. Constitution. In contrast, Butler finds the decisions of Illinois and the U.S. Supreme Court to be in opposition to the intent of the Constitution's framers. Butler argues that Presser and his men were engaging in necessary practice and training as a militia and that the Illinois National Guard of the time was the unconstitutional armed entity.*

If Cruikshank [*United States v. Cruikshank*, 1876] was intended to nullify the Fourteenth Amendment, the State of Illinois intended to nullify a good part of the Second. No, Illinois did not attempt to take away guns. Both the law questioned in *Presser* [*Presser v. Illinois*, 1886] and the opinion of the Court hold that if Congress calls the militia, the people

Bob Butler, "Presser v. Illinois: My Spin," polyticks.com. Reproduced by permission.

must be armed. The state may not interfere with this. However, the state law prevented the militia from drilling, and the court upheld this law.

This is a strange twist on one of the modern gun control arguments. It is said by some gun control advocates that if one is not a trained member of a well drilled militia reporting through proper channels to the state, one has no right to bear arms. The Illinois law discussed in *Presser* forbade the militia from drilling, and eliminated any proper channel for militia to report to the state.

Again, a review of the history of the time is useful.

## Historical Context

Union [Civil War] veterans had a poor view of the militia. Southern militia had killed good men, had pulled units out of action to guard supply lines, but had never really been decisive. Union militia was viewed, perhaps, with even less favor. Northern militia would have fancy uniforms, sleep mostly in their own beds, but were fairly useless in a real fight. Twenty years after . . . [Civil War, 1861–1865] the Union veterans were starting to fill up the state houses. In Illinois, this view of militia as useless turned into a law that forbade the general populace from organizing into military groups. It also established the Illinois National Guard, limited in size to 8000 men, that would train to regular army standard.

Strictly speaking, the Illinois National Guard in question was not the modern National Guard. It was a state guard, paid by the state, reporting to the governor, with no responsibility to federal chain of command. (The modern National Guard, paid for and reporting to the federal government, was not formed until 1905.) As such, the Illinois National Guard was unconstitutional. Illinois had not requested permission from Congress to raise troops. I suspect they had just not bothered. I suspect Congress would have given permission had they thought to ask.

# Details of the Case

While the Illinois law reflected American experience in the Civil War, Presser was an immigrant from Europe, from Germany. Their recent war experience was the Franco-Prussian War [1870–1871]. While the United States might not remember its recent war fondly, or see a major war in its future, Germany and France were both anticipating a rematch. The entire fit adult male populations of both countries were either active military or reserves. The massive mobilization plans that would in time be used to start the First World War [1914–1918] were already being prepared and practiced.

Presser and two hundred other enthusiastic members of the Lehr und Wehr Verein military company thus thought it their patriotic duty to be ready to support their country under arms. This brought them head on against the State of Illinois. Illinois didn't want citizens trained, armed, and organized.

Presser was fined $10. He appealed that fine all the way to the Supreme Court.

> A well regulated Militia, being necessary to the security of a free State, the right of the people to keep and bear arms, shall not be infinged.

This case is about a body of men trying to make themselves ready to contribute to the security of a free State, a state which forbade them from doing so, and a Supreme Court that upheld the state. In the opinion of the court, one's duty as a member of the militia can be met by keeping a weapon ready in case the federal government should call. Training to be ready to use that weapon as part of a coordinated team is not related to one's duty to the federal government. The state may properly forbid such training.

Right.

The logic used is similar to that of *Cruikshank*. The right to assemble isn't valid unless one is petitioning for redress of grievances or performing another function specified in the Constitution. Training for militia duty is not a function specified in the Constitution. Organizing into a military company is not an immunity or privilege of U.S. citizens, therefore the Fourteenth Amendment does not forbid the states from legislating on such subjects. Thus, the well regulated Militia, though necessary to the security of a free State, was outlawed in Illinois. I'm sure this wasn't the intent of the founding fathers. I know, the Fourteenth and First amendment aspects of *Presser* would not stand in a modern court. Still, as no case has been brought before the Court to contradict this one, it still stands.

# CHAPTER 2

# The Supreme Court Addresses the Second Amendment

# Chapter Preface

## Case Overview: *United States v. Miller* (1939)

The case of *United States v. Miller* made its way to the U.S. Supreme Court after the U.S District Court for the Western District of Arkansas quashed the indictment against Jack Miller and Frank Layton for possessing and transporting a sawed-off shotgun, without registering the weapon or paying the required tax, in violation of the National Firearms Act of 1934. The district court found that the law itself was in violation of the Second Amendment, and the government appealed.

The National Firearms Act required that any shotgun with a barrel less than eighteen inches long (among other criteria) be officially registered and that the owner pay a tax—a tax that was, in fact, high enough to often be considered prohibitive. Seemingly, the act sought to limit gun violence by limiting the ability of people to carry concealed weapons. Miller and Layton, who were under surveillance because of being suspected in crimes, transported the unregistered shotgun at issue from Oklahoma to Arkansas and were thus arrested. U.S. District Court Judge Heartsill Ragon concluded, in agreement with Miller's attorneys, that the National Firearms Act was an attempt to "usurp police power reserved to the States" and was unconstitutional under the Second Amendment.

The U.S. Supreme Court disagreed with Ragon on this point but nevertheless handed down an ambiguous ruling that in the years since has been interpreted various ways. In the Court's opinion, Justice McReynolds wrote that because there was no evidence that Miller's shotgun, with a barrel less than eighteen inches long, had any relationship to the militia, the Court "cannot say" that the Second Amendment guaranteed Miller the right to keep and bear the firearm. The Court opinion proceeds to discuss the purposes of and expectations for militias and their members at length.

The Court's focus on the firearm's possible relationship to militia use is one aspect of the ruling that created, and has continued to create, confusion and debate. Many gun-control advocates see this ruling as an affirmation of the government's ability to restrict individual ownership of firearms particularly when said firearms are not specifically owned for use in the militia. Some of their opponents, however, argue that the Court's emphasis on the length of the shotgun barrel and its nonmilitary status indicates that weapons suitable for military use *are* protected—a position very much the opposite of the one taken by gun-control advocates, who see such military-grade weapons as those that should be even more *greatly* restricted. Not surprisingly, litigants, attorneys, politicians, and lobbyists on both sides of the issue have cited *Miller*, the only U.S. Supreme Court case to directly address the confusion over the Second Amendment, interpreting the ruling in very different ways.

"Most . . . States have adopted provisions touching the right to keep and bear arms. . . . But none . . . afford any material support for the challenged ruling of the court below."

# The Court's Decision: The National Firearms Act Does Not Violate the Constitution

## Justice James Clark McReynolds

*Justice James Clark McReynolds, a Kentucky native, received his law degree from the University of Virginia Law School in 1884. After practicing law in Nashville, Tennessee, for several years, McReynolds took an adjunct law professor position at Vanderbilt University in 1900 and stayed there for three years before being appointed, by President Theodore Roosevelt, as the assistant attorney general for the Department of Justice's antitrust division. He returned to law practice in 1907 in New York City. He became Attorney General of the United States in 1913 under President Woodrow Wilson, who subsequently nominated McReynolds to the U.S. Supreme Court in August 1914. McReynolds served on the Court for twenty-six years.*

*In the opinion of the U.S. Supreme Court in the case of* United States v. Miller, *Justice James Clark McReynolds early on in the analysis rules that the National Firearms Act, which Miller was charged with violating, does not usurp police power. Furthermore, there is no evidence that Miller's possession of his shotgun, with a barrel less than eighteen inches in length, was related in*

Justice James Clark McReynolds, majority opinion, *United States v. Miller*, 1939.

*any way to the militia, and thus, McReynolds writes, the Second Amendment does not guarantee Miller's right to bear that arm. McReynolds goes on to discuss, in detail, the Constitution's and states' definitions and intentions for militias before finding that the lower court did not have sufficient support for its decision and reversing the ruling.*

Appeal from the District Court of the United States for the Western District of Arkansas. Mr. Gordon Dean, of Washington, D.C., for the United States.

No appearance for appellees.

Mr. Justice McREYNOLDS delivered the opinion of the Court.

## History of the Case

An indictment in the District Court Western District Arkansas, charged that Jack Miller and Frank Layton "did unlawfully, knowingly, wilfully, and feloniously transport in interstate commerce from the town of Claremore in the State of Oklahoma to the town of Siloam Springs in the State of Arkansas a certain firearm, to-wit, a double barrel 12-gauge Stevens shotgun having a barrel less than 18 inches in length, bearing identification number 76230, said defendants, at the time of so transporting said firearm in interstate commerce as aforesaid, not having registered said firearm as required by Section 1132d of Title 26, United States Code, 26 U.S.C.A. 1132d, and not having in their possession a stamp-affixed written order for said firearm as provided by Section 1132c, Title 26, United States Code, 26 U.S.C.A. 1132c and the regulations issued under authority of the said Act of Congress known as the 'National Firearms Act' approved June 26, 1934, contrary to the form of the statute in such case made and provided, and against the peace and dignity of the United States." A duly interposed demurrer alleged: The National Firearms Act is not a revenue measure but an attempt to usurp police power reserved to the States, and is therefore un-constitutional. Also, it offends the inhibition of the Second Amendment to the Constitution, U.S.C.A.—"A well regulated Militia, being necessary to the security of a free State, the right of the people to keep and bear Arms, shall not be infringed." The District Court held that section 11 of the Act violates the Second Amendment. It accordingly sustained the demurrer and quashed the indictment.

The cause is here by direct appeal.

## The Act Does Not Usurp Police Power

Considering *Sonzinsky v. United States* [1937] and what was ruled in sundry cases arising—under the Harrison Narcotic Act 2—*United States v. Jin Fuey Moy* [1916], *United States v. Doremus* [1919], *Linder v. United States* [1925], *Alston v. United States* [1927], *Nigro v. United States* [1928],—the objection that the Act usurps police power reserved to the States is plainly untenable.

## The Relevance of the Militia to This Case

In the absence of any evidence tending to show that posses-sion or use of a "shotgun having a barrel of less than eighteen inches in length" at this time has some reasonable relationship to the preservation or efficiency of a well regulated militia, we cannot say that the Second Amendment guarantees the right to keep and bear such an instrument. Certainly it is not within judicial notice that this weapon is any part of the ordinary military equipment or that its use could contribute to the common defense. *Aymette v. State of Tennessee.*

## The Constitution's Intent for the Militia

The Constitution as originally adopted granted to the Con-gress power—"To provide for calling forth the Militia to ex-ecute the Laws of the Union, suppress Insurrections and repel Invasions; To provide for organizing, arming, and disciplining, the Militia, and for governing such Part of them as may be employed in the Service of the United States, reserving to the States respectively, the Appointment of the Officers, and the Authority of training the Militia according to the discipline prescribed by Congress." U.S.C.A. Const. art. 1, 8. With obvious purpose to assure the continuation and render possible the effectiveness of such forces the declaration and guarantee of the Second Amendment were made. It must be interpreted and applied with that end in view.

The Militia which the States were expected to maintain and train is set in contrast with Troops which they were forbidden to keep without the consent of Congress. The sentiment of the time strongly disfavored standing armies; the common view was that adequate defense of country and laws could be secured through the Militia—civilians primarily, soldiers on occasion.

## Expectations for the Militia and Its Members

The signification attributed to the term Militia appears from the debates in the Convention, the history and legislation of Colonies and States, and the writings of approved commentators. These show plainly enough that the Militia comprised all males physically capable of acting in concert for the common defense. "A body of citizens enrolled for military discipline." And further, that ordinarily when called for service these men were expected to appear bearing arms supplied by themselves and of the kind in common use at the time.

Blackstone's *Commentaries*, Vol. 2, Ch. 13, p. 409 points out "that king Alfred first settled a national militia in this kingdom" and traces the subsequent development and use of such forces.

Adam Smith's *Wealth of Nations*, Book V. Ch.1, contains an extended account of the Militia. It is there said: "Men of republican principles have been jealous of a standing army as dangerous to liberty." "In a militia, the character of the labourer, artificer, or tradesman, predominates over that of the soldier: in a standing army, that of the soldier predominates over every other character; and in this distinction seems to consist the essential difference between those two different species of military force."

"The American Colonies In The 17th Century", Osgood, Vol. 1, ch. XIII, affirms in reference to the early system of defense in New England.

"In all the colonies, as in England, the militia system was based on the principle of the assize of arms. This implied the general obligation of all adult male inhabitants to possess arms, and, with certain exceptions, to cooperate in the work of defence." "The possession of arms also implied the possession of ammunition, and the authorities paid quite as much attention to the latter as to the former." "A year later (1632) it was ordered that any single man who had not furnished himself with arms might be put out to service, and this became a permanent part of the legislation of the colony (Massachusetts)."

Also "Clauses intended to insure the possession of arms and ammunition by all who were subject to military service appear in all the important enactments concerning military affairs. Fines were the penalty for delinquency, whether of towns or individuals. According to the usage of the times, the infantry of Massachusetts consisted of pikemen and musketeers. The law, as enacted in 1649 and thereafter, provided that each of the former should be armed with a pike, corselet, head-piece, sword, and knapsack. The musketeer should carry a 'good fixed musket,' not under bastard musket bore, not less than three feet, nine inches, nor more than four feet three inches in length, a priming wire, scourer, and mould, a sword, rest, bandoleers, one pound of powder, twenty bullets, and two fathoms of match. The law also required that two-thirds of each company should be musketeers."

## State Laws and Decisions Regarding Militia Requirements for Citizens

The General Court of Massachusetts, January Session 1784, provided for the organization and government of the Militia. It directed that the Train Band should "contain all able bodied men, from sixteen to forty years of age, and the Alarm List, all other men under sixty years of age." Also, "That every non-commissioned officer and private soldier of the said militia not under the controul of parents, masters or guardians, and being of sufficient ability therefor in the judgment of the Selectmen of the town in which he shall dwell, shall equip himself, and be constantly provided with a good fire arm, &c."

By an Act passed April 4, 1786, the New York Legislature directed: "That every able-bodied Male Person, being a Citizen of this State, or of any of the United States, and residing in this State, (except such Persons as are herein after excepted) and who are of the Age of Sixteen, and under the Age of Forty-five Years, shall, by the Captain or commanding Officer of the Beat in which such Citizens shall reside, within four Months after the passing of this Act, be enrolled in the Company of such Beat. . . . That every Citizen so enrolled and notified, shall, within three Months thereafter, provide himself, at his own Expense, with a good Musket or Firelock, a sufficient Bayonet and Belt, a Pouch with a Box therein to contain not less than Twenty-four Cartridges suited to the Bore of his Musket or Firelock, each Cartridge containing a proper Quantity of Powder and Ball, two spare Flints, a Blanket and Knapsack."

The General Assembly of Virginia, October, 1785, declared: "The defense and safety of the commonwealth depend upon having its citizens properly armed and taught the knowledge of military duty."

It further provided for organization and control of the Militia and directed that "All free male persons between the ages of eighteen and fifty years," with certain exceptions, "shall be inrolled or formed into companies." "There shall be a private muster of every company once in two months."

Also that "Every officer and soldier shall appear at his respective muster-field on the day appointed, by eleven o'clock in the forenoon, armed, equipped, and accoutred, as follows: . . . every non-commissioned officer and private with a good, clean musket carrying an ounce ball, and three feet eight inches long in the barrel, with a good bayonet and iron ramrod well fitted thereto, a cartridge box properly made, to contain and secure twenty cartridges fitted to his musket, a good knapsack and canteen, and moreover, each non-commissioned officer and private shall have at every muster one pound of good powder, and four pounds of lead, including twenty blind cartridges; and each serjeant shall have a pair of moulds fit to cast balls for their respective companies, to be purchased by the commanding officer out of the monies arising on delinquencies. Provided, That the militia of the counties westward of the Blue Ridge, and the counties below adjoining thereto, shall not be obliged to be armed with muskets, but may have good rifles with proper accoutrements, in lieu thereof. And every of the said officers, non-commissioned officers, and privates, shall constantly keep the aforesaid arms, accoutrements, and ammunition, ready to be produced whenever called for by his commanding officer. If any private shall make it appear to the satisfaction of the court hereafter to be appointed for trying delinquencies under this act that he is so poor that he cannot purchase the arms herein required, such court shall cause them to be purchased out of the money arising from delinquents."

## Lack of Support for District Court's Decision

Most if not all of the States have adopted provisions touching the right to keep and bear arms. Differences in the language employed in these have naturally led to somewhat variant conclusions concerning the scope of the right guaranteed. But none of them seem to afford any material support for the challenged ruling of the court below.

In the margin some of the more important opinions and comments by writers are cited. We are unable to accept the conclusion of the court below and the challenged judgment must be reversed. The cause will be remanded for further proceedings.

Reversed and remanded.

Mr. Justice took no part in the consideration or decision of this cause.

*"Judges and lawyers, just as much as the Second Amendment revisionists, are caught in the trap of clause-bound, period-bound interpretation."*

# The Fallacy of the Revisionist Approach to Gun Rights

*David Yassky*

*After graduation from Princeton University and Yale Law School, David Yassky practiced law, taught at Brooklyn Law School, and served as chief counsel to the House Subcommittee on Crime, in which position he worked on the Brady law, the Assault Weapons Ban, the Violence Against Women Act, and numerous other anti-crime laws. Since 2001, he has been a member of the New York City Council.*

*In this treatment of Second Amendment history, interpretation, and issues, David Yassky focuses largely on the matter of revisionists. The courts, Yassky states, including the U.S. Supreme Court in* United States v. Miller, *have ruled that the Second Amendment does not preclude the government from enacting gun-control legislation, but revisionist scholars are arguing that the amendment does protect individual gun-ownership rights, as opposed to only rights pertaining to militias. Yassky explores the rise of revisionists and the implications and consequences of their position. He also examines in detail the relationship between New Deal goals and the decisions of the executive and judicial branches with regard to gun control. Yassky dissects and argues against revisionist approaches and also argues that the*

David Yassky, "The Second Amendment: Structure, History, and Constitutional Change," *Michigan Law Review* 99, no. 3 December 2000, pp. 588–668.

*courts have failed to adequately deal with the Second Amendment and the cases that raise Second Amendment issues.*

*A well regulated Militia, being necessary to the security of a free State, the right of the people to keep and bear Arms, shall not be infringed.*

*—United States Constitution, Amendment II*

A fierce debate about the Second Amendment has been percolating in academia for two decades, and has now bubbled through to the courts. The question at the heart of this debate is whether the Amendment restricts the government's ability to regulate the private possession of firearms. Since at least 1939—when the Supreme Court decided *United States v. Miller,* its only decision squarely addressing the scope of the right to "keep and bear Arms"—the answer to that question has been an unqualified "no." Courts have brushed aside Second Amendment challenges to gun control legislation, reading the Amendment to forbid only laws that interfere with states' militias.

## The Emergence of the Revisionist Position

Recently, however, that judicial orthodoxy has come under attack from a group of revisionist scholars. Rather than protecting only the states' militia, the revisionists have argued, the Amendment "protects an individual right inherent in the concept of ordered liberty."

The revisionist position emerged in the 1980s and has won growing acceptance among constitutional scholars. [Note, however, that acceptance of the revisionist argument has for the most part been limited to legal scholars. For the most part, historians have rejected the revisionists' claims.] The breakthrough moment came in 1989, when Stanford Levinson published his article "The Embarassing Second Amendment" in the *Yale Law Journal.* Levinson largely accepted the revisionists' historical account of the Second Amendment, and he suggested that the Amendment limits legislators' ability to regulate guns to a much greater extent than judges and scholars had theretofore acknowledged.

Levinson's article brought the revisionist project a new level of attention and legitimacy. Since its publication, the number of revisionist articles has grown substantially, casebooks have begun to recognize the revisionist position, and other leading constitutional law scholars have joined Levinson in accepting, at least partially, the revisionist argument. In particular, Akhil Amar's recent tour-de-force *The Bill of Rights* [1998] includes a thorough and powerful argument in support of the revisionist position.

## Revisionist Influence on the Judiciary

Most important, revisionist work has begun to influence the judiciary. In his concurring opinion in the 1997 case *Printz v. United States*, Justice [Clarence] Thomas (writing only for himself) proposed a reexamination of the Second Amendment. Thomas suggested that, the Amendment creates a "*personal* right to 'keep and bear arms,'" and he hinted that this right would preclude aggressive gun control regulations.

Just last year [1999] a District Court in Texas followed up on Thomas' suggestion by striking down a federal statute banning persons subject to certain types of restraining orders from possessing firearms. The decision, *United States v. Emerson*, was only the second in the nation's history in which a federal court used the Amendment to invalidate a gun control law (the first was the District Court decision in *Miller* which the Supreme Court subsequently reversed in 1939). Both Justice Thomas' *Printz* opinion and the *Emerson* Court relied heavily on revisionist scholarship.

## The "Embarassing" Second Amendment

The Second Amendment debate sparked by the revisionists has attracted considerable attention in the press, presumably because of its possible impact on public policy. If the revisionists are successful in changing doctrine, courts may well narrow the parameters of permissible gun control initiatives. But paving the way for such initiatives is not my concern here. The real stakes in the Second Amendment debate are not practical, but theoretical.

In his pathbreaking article, Professor Levinson wrote that the Second Amendment is "profoundly embarrassing" to many students of the Constitution. I agree with that characterization, but I disagree with Levinson about the source of the embarrassment. For Levinson, the Amendment calls into question scholars' commitment to result-indifferent interpretive methodology. He noted that the Amendment had (at the time he was writing) been entirely ignored by mainstream constitutional scholars, and he attributed this neglect to a "perhaps subconscious fear that altogether plausible, perhaps even 'winning,' interpretations of the Second Amendment would present real hurdles to those of us supporting prohibitory regulation."

The real source of the embarrassment goes deeper. The Amendment is troublesome because it evokes scholars' latent confusion about the sources and mechanisms of doctrinal change in constitutional law. In particular, the Second Amendment, like no other constitutional provision, puts to the test one's commitment to original intent as a source of constitutional meaning.

Most contemporary scholars, whether they call themselves "originalists" or not, believe that constitutional meaning should be derived, at least in part, from the understandings of those who framed and ratified the constitutional text (or perhaps of the citizens whom those framers and ratifiers represented). The revisionists' argument, which is straightforwardly originalist, poses an uncomfortable challenge to that belief. Their argument, in sum, is this: The framers of the Second Amendment intended for every American citizen to have the right to own guns, free from interference by the federal government; modern courts have approved federal gun control laws that the Founders would certainly have seen as violating the Amendment; accordingly, modern doctrine is illegitimate. . . .

## The Supreme Court's Only Second Amendment Case

The Supreme Court's lone major Second Amendment case, *United States v. Miller*, was decided in 1939—a year after *Carolene Products*, and in the midst of the First Amendment's rebirth. *Miller* involved a prosecution under the National Firearms Act of 1934. This statute, the first federal gun control law, regulated the possession of machineguns and short-barreled shotguns by requiring anyone possessing such a gun to obtain a license from the Treasury Department. Because the licensing process was rigorous and license applicants were required to pay a hefty fee, the effect was a near ban on the private possession of these weapons. As we have seen, a comparable statute enacted in 1800 would surely have been struck down, but the *Miller* Court upheld the law, explicitly rejecting a Second Amendment challenge. There is some debate about the precise meaning of *Miller*—I will say more about this debate below—but at the very least, it is clear that the *Miller* Court avoided giving the Second Amendment a broad construction similar to that of the First. It is indisputable, moreover, that within a few years of *Miller* the lower courts had fleshed out their Organized Militia Approach, and that the Supreme Court has since repeatedly declined to review that approach.

## The Court's Treatment of the First Amendment Under the New Deal

The mystery, then, is why the Court chose not to include the Second Amendment in its resurgent liberty jurisprudence. Without attempting to provide a full-blown explanation of the Court's synthesis of the New Deal [a series of social programs introduced by President Franklin D. Roosevelt during the Great Depression] with pre-existing amendments, let me put forward a working hypothesis: The Supreme Court of the late 1930s and 1940s saw free speech rights as both ameliorating dangers of the new administrative state, while also being rooted in key New Deal themes; accordingly, it revitalized the First Amendment. The Court could not, however, envision a similar role for the right to bear arms.

The main innovation of the New Deal was that it greatly expanded the power of government—and particularly of the federal government. In addition to overturning substantive due process constraints on economic regulation, the Court also eviscerated Commerce Clause and separation of powers restraints on federal power. The cumulative result was a government capable of speedy, sweeping action.

Critics, of course, saw in the new government order a grave threat to individual liberty, and even many New Deal supporters shared this concern, and both groups looked to the Court to set limits. The problem for the Court was to devise limits that would not interfere with the primary aims of the New Deal. The Court's solution was not to restrict the substantive reach of the new administrative state, but to ensure its democratic accountability. The Court saw that because the government could reorder citizens' lives so profoundly, the need for popular control of the government was all the more important. Speech rights were a prime constitutional mechanism for implementing this vision.

The Court's focus on protecting the mechanisms of democratic accountability also helped to resolve a tension within the New Deal's ideological structure. On one hand, [President Franklin D.] Roosevelt's changes were made in the name of majoritarian government. On the other hand, the New Dealers prized "nonpartisan experts" and "independent administrators." And indeed, many critics—and, again, even some friends—of the New Deal believed that the new behemoth government agencies threatened to slip the bonds of majoritarian control. While the Justices' abrogation of the nondelegation doctrine exacerbated this threat, their insistence that political debate remain uncorrupted by government intervention served, in some measure, to alleviate it. Thus by developing a robust, individual right to free speech, the Court elegantly blended constitutional values from the Founding, Reconstruction and the New Deal.

## The Second Amendment Under the New Deal

The Second Amendment picture was quite different. While censorship was no part of Roosevelt's agenda, gun control—as part of crime control—was. The first of his "four freedoms" was "freedom of speech and expression"—the last was "freedom from fear," to be safeguarded by a powerful national government. Indeed, the National Firearms Act upheld in *Miller* was an important component of the New Deal program, and was touted as such in Roosevelt's political speeches. To be sure, the National Firearms Act was not nearly as central to Roosevelt's program as his more well known economic regulation initiatives, but the Act did fit comfortably within his new paradigm of activist central government. To the Justices deciding *Miller* in 1939, striking down the Act would have seemed like a return to the ways of the Old Court. Elevating an individual property right in firearms over the power of the government to promote public welfare would have been wholly inconsistent with New Deal principles.

And if a reconceived (or as Amar would have it, "refined") individual right to own guns fit poorly with the Court's broader post-New Deal jurisprudence, reviving the traditional understanding of the Second Amendment was equally implausible. With another Great War looming, the Founders' preference for state militias over a national army must have seemed quaint to say the least.

## Possible Readings of the Second Amendment

This is not to say, however, that it would have been impossible—or that it is impossible today—for the Court to develop a jurisprudence of the Second Amendment that respects the modern constitutional order. I am not at all sure that the Second Amendment law we have now is the best Second Amendment law we can have, even within interpretively legitimate bounds. Modern doctrine reduces the Amendment to a virtual nullity—and a constitutional amendment is a terrible thing to waste. We cannot, of course, revive the Amendment by returning to the Founders' specific conception of decentralized military structure with states playing an intermediary role. It is another question whether (or to what extent) the core values underlying this structure remain viable. How difficult should it be for the President to use military force? What mechanisms should the Court insist upon—in the name of the Constitution—to ensure that warmaking remains subject to democratic accountability?

Scholars have engaged these questions with some fascinating results. Elaine Scarry, for example, has offered a brilliantly provocative reading in which the Second Amendment prohibits the use of nuclear weapons. David Williams suggests that taking the Second Amendment seriously might mean reviving the universal-service militia. Or perhaps the Second Amendment should be read to *require* a draft—reading the people's right to bear arms, in effect, as a nondelegable duty.

## The Court's Failure to Address the Issue, Even in *Miller*

The courts, however, and most important the Supreme Court, have utterly failed to enter this discussion. We are nearly at the end of this article, and I have said very little about the Supreme Court's opinion in *Miller*. The reason is that the opinion itself says very little. The defendant in the case, Jack Miller, had been prosecuted under the National Firearms Act for unlicensed possession of a short-barreled shotgun, and the Court rejected Miller's Second Amendment challenge to the Act. The operative language in its opinion is this:

> In the absence of any evidence tending to show that possession or use of a "shotgun having a barrel of less than eighteen inches in length" at this time has some reasonable relationship to the preservation or efficiency of a well regulated militia, we cannot say that the Second Amendment guarantees the right to keep and bear such an instrument. Certainly it is not within judicial notice that this weapon is part of the ordinary military equipment or that its use could contribute to the common defense.

## The Revisionists' View of *Miller*

Based on this passage, the revisionists read *Miller* as holding merely that certain weapons are beyond the reach of Second Amendment protection. They contend that lower courts have illegitimately constructed the Organized Militia Approach by taking *Miller*'s language about "the preservation of efficiency of a well regulated militia" out of context.

There are problems with the revisionists' view of *Miller*. First, the National Firearms Act regulated not only short-barreled shotguns but also machine guns—which were standard-issue military equipment in 1939, as they are today. The *Miller* Court does not even mention that fact. Yet if we read *Miller* as resting on the premise that short-barreled shotguns are not "military equipment," the National Firearms Act's regulation of machine guns is presumably unconstitutional. True, judges are supposed to limit themselves to the case at hand, but it seems odd that the Court would have upheld one part of a statute by formulating a rule that immediately and obviously invalidates another part of the very same statute without even alluding to the tension.

Second, the revisionist reading of *Miller* has the perverse result that the deadlier a firearm is, the more likely it is to receive constitutional protection—because the military, of course, prefers weapons that are as efficient and effective at killing as possible. Or as the First Circuit put it in a case decided a few years after *Miller* [*Cases v. United States*]: "Another objection [to this reading of *Miller*] . . . is that according to it Congress would be prevented by the Second Amendment from regulating the possession or use by private persons . . . of distinctly military arms, such as machine guns, trench mortars, anti-tank or anti-aircraft guns."

Moreover, the *Miller* opinion does plainly rule out the revisionists' Libertarian Approach. If the Second Amendment is truly about a personal right to arm oneself, then the question whether there is any link between the regulated weapon and militia service, the question at the crux of *Miller*, is irrelevant. A sawed-off shotgun is quite useful for self-defense—it is, in fact, a terrifying weapon—and under the Libertarian Approach, denying access to such a weapon would certainly infringe upon a protected Second Amendment interest.

## The Reasons Behind the Courts' Readings of *Miller*

These are all good reasons to reject the revisionists' reading of *Miller*. But I believe the most important reason courts have read *Miller* the way they have is because they sense the importance of the changes in constitutional structure that I have tried to examine in this article. The Organized Militia Approach should be seen as an effort to understand the "right to keep and bear Arms" in light of the Fourteenth Amendment's radical shift of power—including military power—from the states to the federal government. The Founders designed the Constitution in the belief that state militias were preferable to a federal army; after the Civil War, this belief could no longer serve as a fundamental constitutional premise. By the time *Miller* reached the Court, it had been twenty years since the *Selective Draft Law Cases* approved a federal draft, confirming the repudiation of Article I's protections for the militia. The purpose of the Second Amendment had been to fortify the Militia Clauses; now that these provisions were a dead letter, the Second Amendment was adrift.

## Reasons for and Results of the Courts' Failure

But I concede, as I must, that neither *Miller* nor the lower court opinions building on it give any hint of these historical and structural concerns. This failure has significant costs. Not only has the opportunity to develop meaningful Second Amendment doctrine gone unrealized, but the Amendment's role in public debate has become distorted. Over the past two years [1998–2000] for example, Congress has debated a series of gun control measures advanced in the wake of the Columbine tragedy. During the same period, Congress also considered a resolution essentially reaffirming the War Powers Resolution, proposed in the context of major commitments of U.S. military personnel in the Middle East and in Bosnia. Senators and Representatives referred repeatedly to the Second Amendment in opposing the gun control provisions, the Amendment was not mentioned once in reference to the military.

But while the courts' failure is costly, it should not seem surprising, as the method of constitutional interpretation I am advocating is sharply at variance with contemporary practice. Judges and lawyers, just as much as the Second Amendment revisionists, are caught in the trap of clause-bound, period-bound interpretation. Only by adopting a textually holistic and historically sensitive methodology can we uncover the reasons behind the disappearance of the Second Amendment and begin to think constructively about whether, and how, to revive it.

*"Yassky's reading of* Miller *is mistaken. . . . [T]he decision is best understood as leaving open the opportunity for courts to adopt the Standard Model reading of the Second Amendment."*

# The Protection of an Individual's Right to Keep and Bear Arms

## Brannon P. Denning and Glenn H. Reynolds

*Brannon P. Denning is assistant professor of law at Southern Illinois University in Carbondale. Glenn H. Reynolds is professor of law at the University of Tennessee in Knoxville.*

*In the following essay, professors Brannon P. Denning and Glen H. Reynolds discuss at length* United States v. Miller, *arguing that the case provides the basis for the Standard Model, or individual-rights interpretation, of the Second Amendment, which contends that the Constitution protects an individual's right to bear arms. They focus on David Yassky's essay in the December 2000* Michigan Law Review *in which he purports that the* Miller *case does not support what he labels the "Libertarian Approach" to the Second Amendment. They conclude that the* Miller *decision endorses the individual-rights model.*

Only in recent years have those opposed to the individual rights interpretation of the Second Amendment [that the right to keep and bear arms belongs to individuals], which one of us dubbed the "Standard Model," come forth with theories attempting to harmonize text, history, and structure to show that the Amendment is the Constitution's version of Oakland—that there is no "there" there [referring to a famous quote by writer Gertrude Stein about her hometown of Oakland, California]. Earlier "theories" had tended to be merely makeweight arguments whose implications were never probed in depth by their proponents. A recent article by Professor David Yassky [in December 2000] suggests that there is a segment of legal academia that dissents from the Standard Model and has started to generate alternatives to the Standard Model. In this brief essay, we critique that part of Yassky's theory dismissing *United States v. Miller* [1939] as providing the basis for an individual rights interpretation of the Second Amenment.

## Yassky's Response

In his provocative response to the Standard Model, Yassky argues that, if the dramatic changes to our constitutional regime since the time of the Amendment's drafting are taken into account, the Standard Model proves inadequate. One question that Yassky addresses is why the Supreme Court has continued to underenforce the Amendment, treating it as a "constitutional pariah, barred from associating with other 'high caste' civil liberties that [the Court] has labored to protect" in the years since the so-called Constitutional Revolution of 1937. Yassky provides this answer:

> The Supreme Court of the late 1930s and 1940s saw [civil liberties like freedom of speech] as both ameliorating dangers of the new administrative state, while also being rooted in key New Deal themes [such as Roosevelt's famous "Four Freedoms"]; accordingly it revitalized the First Amendment. The court could not, however, envision a similar role for the right to keep and bear arms.

## *United States v. Miller*

This, Yassky argues, is key to understanding what he terms "the failure of the courts" to enforce the Amendment and accounts for its virtual repeal at all levels of the federal judiciary. Indicative of this failure is the United States Supreme Court's only case this century squarely addressing the Second Amendment, *United States v. Miller*. Yassky, however, devotes only a few pages to *Miller*, a decision he defends only with the observation that the opinion "says very little." What he does say is that "the *Miller* opinion . . . plainly rule[s] out" what he terms "the revisionists' Libertarian Approach" to the Second Amendment.

## Yassky's Argument

Yassky's reading of *Miller* is mistaken. When the decision is read closely and the arguments available (and not available) to the Court are taken into account, the decision is best understood as leaving open the opportunity for courts to adopt the Standard Model reading of the Second Amendment. What *Miller* plainly does *not* do is deny that an individual's right to keep and bear arms is protected by the Second Amendment—the holding ascribed to it by most federal courts since 1939. Yassky's error on this subject requires correction.

At the outset, we admit that we are focusing on a small part of Yassky's argument, but we think that this focus on *Miller* is justifiable on several grounds. First, any subsequent Supreme Court interpretation of the Second Amendment will have to take *Miller* into account. It is *Miller*, after all, that lower courts have cited to maintain that the Second Amendment did not create an individual right to keep and bear arms. If Yassky is correct and the Standard Model or "Libertarian Approach" finds no support there, then that would likely end the matter for courts. They would have no need to resort to Yassky's elaborate arguments that dramatic shifts in military posture, begun in the nineteenth century and completed in the twentieth, from state militia to a federally controlled, professional military apparatus constitute a temporally extended "constitutional moment" that has drained the Second Amendment of enforceable content.

On the other hand, if, as we argue, *Miller* does not close the door on the enforcement of the Second Amendment, then that, too, is important. While a Supreme Court endorsement of the Standard Model does not settle the scope of the right, it does move the debate beyond the point at which it is presently stalled: the question whether it guarantees any individual right at all. A judicial victory for the Standard Model would also be a rebuke to lower courts that have consistently overread *Miller*. Recognizing an individual right would then, of necessity, move the debate to questions about the scope of the right: the legitimacy of the government's interest in controlling individual possession of certain types of weapons, the reasonableness of particular gun control proposals, the availability of less restrictive alternatives, and the like. All are questions that form the warp and woof of ordinary constitutional law. That we are still mired in questions of the Second Amendment's applicability to individuals suggests how primitive our Second Amendment "jurisprudence" is. No one seriously makes arguments to the courts, for example, that the First Amendment protects a "collective right" to the free exchange of political ideas and was never intended to cover the myriad forms of individual expressive activity that find protection in the Supreme Court's decisions.

## The Supreme Court's Holding in
## *United States v. Miller*

*United States v. Miller* arose as a result of an appeal taken by the United States Government to the Supreme Court following the dismissal of an indictment against two Arkansas men accused of possessing a sawed-off shotgun in violation of the National Firearms Act of 1934. The U.S. District Court for the

Western District of Arkansas had quashed the indictment, finding that the National Firearms Act "offend[ed] the inhibition of the Second Amendment to the Constitution." The government appealed directly to the United States Supreme Court. The government was the only party that filed a brief with the Court and was the sole party appearing at oral argument.

The Supreme Court reversed the District Court, but in doing so, it avoided any sweeping statements regarding the scope of the Second Amendment. It simply held that

> [i]n the absence of any evidence tending to show that possession or use of a [sawed-off shotgun] at this time has some reasonable relationship to the preservation or efficiency of a well regulated militia, we cannot say that the Second Amendment guarantees the right to keep and bear such an instrument. Certainly it is not within judicial notice that this weapon is any part of the ordinary military equipment or that its use could contribute to the common defense.

Implicit in the holding is that if the defendants *had* made such a showing, the Court might have struck down the provision in question. Moreover, there seemed no question that the defendants as individuals were competent to raise the Second Amendment as a defense. If a collective or states' rights view were adopted, the Court could have reversed the District Court on the ground that the individual defendants—who were quite obviously not "states," and who apparently were not members of any formal or informal "well regulated militia"—did not have standing to invoke the Second Amendment's protections. That it did not question the defendants' standing strongly suggests that the Court did not adopt a "states' rights" or "collective rights" interpretation of the Second Amendment.

While Justice [James Clark] McReynolds described the "obvious purpose" of the Second Amendment as assuring the continuing effectiveness of the militia, and wrote that the Amendment "must be interpreted and applied with that end in view," he also noted that, at the time of the Framing, militias were made up of individuals—"all males physically capable of acting in concert for the common defense" who often supplied their own weapons. Militia members are, in Justice McReynolds's words, "civilians primarily, soldiers on occasion." More importantly, they are, as McReynolds recognized, *individuals*. Securing for individuals the right to keep and bear arms enabled them to serve as members of militias, thus providing the primary means of "assur[ing] the continuation and render[ing] possible the effectiveness of" militias. As Thomas Cooley noted, "[t]he alternative to a standing army is a 'well-regulated militia'; but this cannot exist unless the people are trained to bearing arms."

## The *Miller* Court and the Government's Argument

Further supporting the argument that the *Miller* Court implicitly adopted an individual rights interpretation of the Second Amendment is the fact that the Court rejected the collective rights argument made by the United States Government in its brief.

The government claimed that "the very language of the Second Amendment discloses that this right has reference only to the keeping and bearing of arms by the people as members of the state militia or other similar military organizations provided for by law." The government further argued that the Second Amendment "gave sanction only to the arming of the people as a body to defend their rights against tyrannical and unprincipled rulers" and "did not permit the keeping of arms for purposes of private defense." The reference to a "well regulated militia" that precedes the Second Amendment, it maintained, "indicates that the right to keep and bear arms is not one which may be utilized for private purposes but only one which exists where the arms are borne in the militia or some other military organization provided for by law and intended for the protection of the state."

## Military Arms or Weapons

The Court made no direct mention of these arguments in its opinion; instead, it partially adopted another of the government's arguments. Assuming *arguendo* that the Second Amendment protects an individual right to keep and bear arms, the government argued, the only arms protected were those suitable to military purposes, as opposed to weapons—like sawed-off shotguns—that "constitute the arsenal of the 'public enemy' and the 'gangster'" and that the National Firearms Act was intended to regulate. Even here the Court handed the government only half a loaf. The *Miller* Court said merely that it was presented with no evidence of, and could not take judicial notice of, a sawed-off shotgun's military utility.

It is true that "[t]he Court [in *Miller*] did not . . . attempt to define, or otherwise construe, the substantive right protected by the Second Amendment." It is also true, however, that *Miller* could be read to have adopted the Standard Model: (1) by not reversing the lower court's decision on the ground that the defendants lacked standing; and (2) by rejecting the government's arguments that the Second Amendment protected only a collective right.

## Yassky's Narrow Reading of *Miller*

In his article, Yassky states that "the *Miller* opinion does plainly rule out the revisionists' Libertarian Approach." Despite the certitude with which he makes this claim, the evidence he posits in support of it is meager, and his arguments belie an unfamiliarity with those put forth by the government in *Miller*. First, he claims that "revisionists read *Miller* as holding merely that certain weapons are beyond the reach of Second Amendment protection" based on certain language, such as the

Court's refusal to take judicial notice of a sawed-off shotgun's military utility. This is a problem, he argues, because the National Firearms Act also regulated machine guns, which, he claims, "were standard-issue military equipment in 1939, as they are today." Yassky explains that, "if we read *Miller* as resting on the premise that short-barreled shotguns are not 'military equipment,' the National Firearms Act's regulation of machine guns is presumably unconstitutional." Even allowing for the fact that "judges are supposed to limit themselves to the case at hand," he is incredulous at the possibility that "the Court would have upheld one part of the statute by formulating a rule that immediately and obviously invalidates another part of the very same statute without even alluding to the tension."

His conclusion is flawed for several reasons. First, the government itself proffered the "military utility" argument. If the government failed to note the tension Yassky sees, then why should it bother the Court? Second, Yassky's conclusion is based on the erroneous premise that *Miller* was indeed establishing a rule, or that, if it did, that that rule "immediately and obviously" invalidated anything. Recall that the Court said only that it could not take "judicial notice" of the fact that the shotgun was part of standard military equipment or somehow militarily useful. The Court's statement was simply an acknowledgment of the fact that it had seen no conclusive evidence one way or the other. And how could it have? The government was the only party who appeared before the Court at oral argument, and the only party who filed a brief in the case. Assuming that the Court did intend to set a threshold requirement of military utility for Second Amendment protection, as many state courts had under analogous state constitutional provisions, it does not follow that the government's regulation of machine guns under the National Firearms Act would be *prima facie* unconstitutional. Instead, it might merely mean that, in modern Supreme Court parlance, government regulation of such weapons must survive strict scrutiny—the regulations must serve a compelling governmental interest and be narrowly tailored to serve that interest. Of course, since strict scrutiny has been described as "'strict' in theory but fatal in fact," its application to legislation regulating private gun ownership could presage a more libertarian reading of the Second Amendment by courts—that is, an interpretation of the Amendment that is more hostile to some forms of gun control.

## *Miller* and the Individual's Possession of Arms

We cannot know what the Court would have done had sufficient evidence been presented. The Court framed its decision only in terms of information that it did not have. But it did not hold, as the government urged, that the Second Amendment did not protect an individual right. At the very least, *Miller* suggests that the Court was open to such arguments and that weapons with military utility could find protection under the Second Amendment, with the burden shifting to the government to demonstrate why its regulation of such weapons is necessary and reasonable.

Yassky further argues that a "revisionist reading of *Miller* has the perverse result that the deadlier a firearm is, the more likely it is to receive constitutional protection—because the military . . . prefers weapons that are as efficient and effective at killing as possible." This argument echoes the favored *reductio ad absurdum* of courts and anti-Standard Model scholars alike: that an individual rights reading of the Second Amendment would compel judicial protection for individual possession of nuclear weapons. Yassky quotes from a sixty-year-old First Circuit opinion, *Cases v. United States*, which speculated that *Miller*, taken to its logical conclusion, would require protection for individual possession of "distinctly military arms, such as machine guns, trench mortars, anti-tank or anti-aircraft guns. . . ." The point, however, is a *non sequitur*. Recognizing the existence of an individual right under the Second Amendment and the articulation of the right's scope are separate issues. It does not follow from the former that a court would be obliged to countenance any individual's possession of any sort of weapon, any more than the right to free speech protects offers to bribe government officials.

## The Libertarian Approach

Finally, Yassky states that, if the crux of *Miller* is the "link between the regulated weapon and militia service," then the Second Amendment cannot "truly [be] about a personal right to arm oneself," because a sawed-off shotgun "is quite useful for self-defense—it is, in fact, a terrifying weapon—and under the Libertarian Approach, denying access to such a weapon would certainly infringe upon a Second Amendment interest." First, to the extent that he suggests that those endorsing a Libertarian Approach—what we term the Standard Model—oppose any and all forms of gun control, Yassky's argument is a red herring. That is not how he initially described the Libertarian Approach in his article and is not the position of Standard Modelers, whose views on the scope of permissible regulation of private ownership of firearms vary widely, but who generally accept a degree of regulation as legitimate. Moreover, it suggests that accepting the Standard Model requires elevating the personal right of self-defense over all other competing societal claims. Early state court decisions interpreting state constitutional provisions rejected the idea that these views were mutually exclusive. These decisions allowed individuals to carry certain weapons for self-defense including those useful for military service, like revolvers, while banning certain weapons like derringers, stilettos, and Bowie Knives that could be concealed; they also, for the most part, upheld bans outlawing the public carrying of concealed weapons.

In his article, Yassky creates a false dichotomy. The Second Amendment has to guarantee either a personal right of self-defense or a right bound up with obligations to perform, at least part time, military service for "collective" self-defense. He ignores a third possibility that Don Kates has explored: that the Framer's vision for the universal militia—a collection of citizen-soldiers coming to the defense of each other, or the state, against invasion or usurpation—was merely the widely acknowledged right—obligation, even—of personal self-defense, against criminals for instance, writ large.

## *Miller* Supports the Standard Model

Despite a spirited effort to rehabilitate *Miller*'s treatment at the hands of the lower federal courts, Yassky falls short. His reading of *Miller* is not persuasive. Moreover, his account fails to take into consideration the arguments that were *not* adopted by the Court in rendering the *Miller* decision. From the perspective of gun control proponents, *Miller* is, at best, agnostic on the question of the Second Amendment's guarantee of an individual right. When, however, the decision is read in context, recognizing that the government was the only side arguing the case and that many of its main arguments were apparently rejected, or at least not adopted, by the Court, the decision begins to look more hospitable to a Standard Model reading.

## The Courts Failed to Read *Miller* Carefully

What is clear from reading *Miller* is that what Yassky perceives as a "failure of the courts" is not a failure to recognize a constitutional moment, but rather a failure at a more basic level: the failure to read *Miller* carefully and apply it as they would any other somewhat vague Supreme Court decision. Instead, lower court judges have invoked the Supreme Court's recognized authority to "declare what the law is" to silence judicial dialogue; implicit in their opinions is the feeling that the Second Amendment ought not to exist. Yassky may be correct that judges had a hard time finding a place for the right after the New Deal, or that a fundamental alteration in national defense policy made it difficult to account for the reference to a "militia" being "necessary for the security of a free state," but that is no warrant for a continued attempt to read the Second Amendment out of the Bill of Rights. Or even out of *Miller*.

*"The [cases'] details . . . vary, yet the decisions reached in all of them fundamentally affirm that the Constitution does not limit the states' ability to restrict private gun ownership."*

# Gun-Control Measures Support the Court's Interpretation of the Second Amendment

*Amitai Etzioni*

*Amitai Etzioni, who received his PhD in sociology from the University of California–Berkeley in 1958, spent twenty years as a professor at Columbia University, including time as the department chair. In 1979 he was recruited to be the senior adviser on domestic affairs to the White House, and in 1980 he became the first University Professor at George Washington University. He also founded both the Society for the Advancement of Socio-Economics and the nonprofit, nonpartisan Communitarian Network. In addition to having published two dozen books, Etzioni edited* The Responsive Community: Rights and Responsibilities *from 1991 to 2004. He is the director of the Institute for Communitarian Policy Studies at George Washington University.*

*Here, Amitai Etzioni argues that the courts have been clear that the Constitution does not bar states from restricting gun rights, but that opponents of this view have been trying to "erode the long-standing interpretation of the Second Amendment." He out-*

Amitai Etzioni, "Reasonable Regulation," *National Law Journal*, vol. 26, April 5, 2004. Copyright © 2004 American Lawyer Media L.P. Reproduced by permission.

*lines how the National Rifle Association and some politicians have worked to undermine gun-control legislation and touches on some recent relevant cases.*

Most of the attention that has recently been paid to guns has focused on extending the ban on assault weapons, continuing to conduct background checks, and protecting the gun industry from liability for consequences flowing from the use of its dangerous products. Much more attention should be paid to the attempts to erode the long-standing interpretation of the Second Amendment.

The Second Amendment is often referred to simply as "a right to bear arms." Actually, . . . the full text reads, "A well regulated Militia, being necessary to the security of a free State, the right of the people to keep and bear Arms, shall not be infringed." Still, whenever this issue has reached the high court, in cases spanning nearly 125 years, the court has ruled that there is no constitutional barrier to limiting or removing guns owned by individuals.

When one reads the relevant case law, from as early as 1875 (*United States v. Cruikshank*) to 1997 (*Printz v. United States*), the details of the cases vary, yet the decisions reached in all of them fundamentally affirm that the Constitution does not limit the states' ability to restrict private gun ownership. Consider the oft-cited *United States v. Miller* (1939). Jack Miller had not properly registered his sawed-off shotgun or paid a tax for transporting the weapon across state lines, as required under the 1934 Firearms Act. Miller claimed that the act violated his Second Amendment rights. The Court ruled that because Miller could not prove that his shotgun had "some reasonable relationship to the preservation or efficiency of a well-regulated militia, it cannot be said that the Second Amendment to the Federal Constitution guarantees the right to keep and bear such an instrument, or that the [act] violates [the Constitution]."

## Fighting Words

Miller and its antecedents seem plain enough. But, when I posted an overview of these cases on a Web page, it unleashed a storm of criticism. Among the many cuss words, several counterarguments were raised. Correspondents quoted Washington, Jefferson, Madison and George Mason to show that our founding fathers were proponents of private gun ownership. My response was that ours is a government of laws, which cannot be trumped by quotations from even the most important American icons.

The National Rifle Association (NRA), as a rule, does not challenge gun control laws before the Supreme Court—it knows what the outcome will be. Others have argued that we should not be bound in such arguments by what the Supreme Court states, as it can be wrong and even overrule itself. Fair enough. However, if we are not going to accept 125 years of consistent rulings as the legal standard, then what shall we rely on?

## Recent Court Decisions

The challenge to the long-standing interpretation of the Second Amendment is coming from a combination of recent court decisions and the attorney general's [in 2004] strong support for the NRA. Several years ago, the high court declined to review a decision of the 5th U.S. Circuit Court of Appeals in *United States v. Emerson* [2001]. The case concerned Timothy Emerson, who was found guilty of possessing a firearm while subject to a court order prohibiting him from threatening his wife. The court ruled against Emerson, but supported his individual right to bear arms (arguing only that the government could restrict that right with "limited, narrowly tailored specific exceptions or restrictions"). In deciding not to hear the case, the Supreme Court, for the first time, allowed an individualized interpretation of the Second Amendment to stand, an interpretation that has the enthusiastic support of [former] Attorney General John Ashcroft. Meanwhile, the Supreme Court also recently declined to hear the case of *Silveira v. Lockyer,* in which the 9th Circuit ruled that the Constitution "does not provide any type of individual right to own or possess weapons." Where we go from here is one more important issue whose resolution will clearly depend on the outcome of the upcoming presidential and congressional elections.

## Guns Make It Easier to Kill

As someone who served as a commando for 2 1/2 years, I hate and fear guns. It is true, as the NRA argues, that criminals (rather than guns) kill people, but it is also true that guns make it much easier for criminals to do so. No one standing atop the clock tower at the University of Texas could have killed 17 people and wounded 31 using knives or wrenches, to give but one example. And thousands of children die each year from the accidental discharge of firearms.

Guns are not the only thing that affects my vote, but you will not find it difficult to guess in which direction they are pointing me.

*"Whether the right is viewed as embarrassing, terrifying, or as an essential means to individual liberty and personal autonomy, the fact of the right's existence remains."*

# Second Amendment Scholarship and the Individual Rights Interpretation

*Jerry Bonanno*

*Jerry Bonanno worked in the environmental compliance and radiation safety fields, with a degree in environmental sciences, before earning a master's in public health and subsequently his JD from Seton Hall University School of Law. After receiving his law degree in 2005. Bonanno joined the United States Nuclear Regulatory Commission as an attorney.*

*In this in-depth analysis of Second Amendment history and scholarship, Jerry Bonanno covers a wide range of topics beginning with the international push for civilian disarmament that the United States has resisted. He goes on to describe the internal debate over gun control within the United States and delineates the differences between two models of Second Amendment interpretation: the standard model and the collective rights model. After exploring the possible meanings behind and historical context of the terminology used in the Second Amendment and looking at U.S. v.* Miller, *which he notes did not come down*

Jerry Bonanno, "Facing the Lion in the Bush: Exploring the Implications of Adopting an Individual Rights Interpretation of the Second Amendment to the United States Constitution," *Hamline Law Review*, vol. 29, 2006, p. 463-500. Copyright © 2006 by Hamline Law Review. Reproduced by permission.

*fully on either side of the debate, Bonanno concludes that there is a "unique relationship between firearms and the American citizen" and that the right is indeed a right, one that the United States should focus on further clarifying and defining rather than arguing over its existence.*

In July of 2001, the United Nations Conference on the Illicit Trade in Small Arms and Light Weapons in All Its Aspects, ("Conference") was held in New York City. The Conference was convened to work toward a global non-proliferation regime for small arms and light weapons, which United Nations Secretary-General Kofi Annan described as "weapons of mass destruction." At the conclusion of the meeting, the President of the Conference issued the following statement:

> While congratulating all participants for their diligence in reaching this new consensus, I must, as President, also express my disappointment over the Conference's inability to agree, due to the concerns of one State, on language recognizing the need to establish and maintain controls over private ownership of these deadly weapons [small arms and light weapons] and the need for preventing sales of such arms to non-State groups.

The State referenced in the statement is the United States of America, and the "deadly weapons" referred to include "small arms," such as revolvers, self-loading pistols and rifles. John R. Bolton, who was at the time the United States Under Secretary of State for Arms Control and International Security, expressed the United States' concerns in a statement issued to the Conference on July 9, 2001. In his statement, Under Secretary Bolton expressed specific concern over measures prohibiting civilian possession of small arms. Under Secretary Bolton went on to state that "[t]he United States will not join consensus on a final document that contains measures abrogating the Constitutional right to bear arms." The Constitutional right to keep and bear arms is enumerated in the Second Amendment to the United States Constitution.

## The Debate within the United States

In addition to the international push for disarmament of civilian populations, the Second Amendment has come under attack by members of the press, politicians, government commissions, academics, medical researchers, judges, and the anti-gun lobby. They argue that the United States should adopt strict gun control laws modeled after the regimes of foreign democracies. This global peer pressure to restrict the right of civilians to possess firearms, coupled with the United States Supreme Court's extremely limited treatment of the Second Amendment, provides additional incentive to delineate the contours of the right to keep and bear arms. However, in order to develop an analytical framework that would allow for constitutional scrutiny of gun control proposals on both the international and domestic levels, consensus must first be reached on what, if anything, the Second Amendment protects.

Along these lines, there has been much academic debate over the past twenty years regarding the meaning of the Second Amendment. Two primary interpretive theories have emerged from this debate. These theories are the "standard model" (individual rights model) and the "collective rights model." Although recent research has revealed many more United States Supreme Court cases dealing with firearms use and ownership than previously cited in legal scholarship, the Court's most direct treatment of the Amendment took place in 1939. Since that time, the debate over the extent to which the Second Amendment protects an individual's right to own firearms, and the effect that the conclusions drawn from that debate will have on the ability of the state and federal governments to impose limits on private ownership of firearms, has escalated.

## What Does the Second Amendment Mean?

To this point, much of the scholarly debate has rightly focused on determining the original meaning of the Second Amendment. Although this scholarship has yielded several plausible interpretations of the Amendment, the general consensus among legal scholars is that the Second Amendment protects an individual's right to own firearms. In addition, the most recent official opinion issued by the United States Department of Justice recognizes that the Second Amendment protects an individual's right to own firearms. Running concurrent with, and often indistinguishable from, the legal debate over the Second Amendment is the collateral, and often bitter, debate over gun control policy. In this public policy debate, the most common objection to a strong individual rights reading of the Second Amendment is that recognizing a fundamental individual right to own firearms is simply too dangerous. The theme of prohibitive societal danger associated with recognizing an individual's right to own firearms is also prevalent in the academic debate over the nature of the right protected by the Second Amendment. Social costs aside, commentators have also made insightful, compelling arguments that the modern gun control debate has little to do with either the Constitution or crime control.

As a practical matter, a Supreme Court decision simply adopting an individual rights reading of the Second Amendment would be analogous to a ship's captain spotting the tip of an iceberg. Certainly, such a decision would create "a swarm of much more difficult questions." This comment will address some of those questions by exploring the legal consequences of recognizing that the Second Amendment protects an individual's right to keep and bear firearms, unrelated to any state-sanctioned militia service. Specifically, this comment will build on other scholarly work that has attempted to develop a functional analytical framework for evaluating Second Amendment challenges to gun control legislation. . . .

## Second Amendment Scholarship

The scholarship dedicated to deciphering the Second Amendment is extensive and a complete review of the literature is outside the scope of this comment. The summary of the interpretative theories provided is necessarily abbreviated and simply meant to provide context for the subsequent discussion of adopting an individual rights reading of the Amendment.

*The Collective Rights Interpretation* Although there is more than one version of what can be categorized as the collective rights interpretation of the Second Amendment, the end result of any of these interpretations is that the Second Amendment protects little, if anything, of modern importance. Specifically, the states' right interpretation construes the Amendment as protecting only a state's right to arm and field a well regulated militia. Under this interpretation, an individual citizen simply has no constitutionally protected right keep or bear arms. More nuanced collective readings of the Amendment concede that there may be an individual right to keep and bear arms, but limit that right to possession of arms for the civic purpose of service in state militias.

Although these theories differ to some extent, barring the reinvigoration of the general citizen militia, the end result of adopting them is to render the Second Amendment a dead letter. In summary, these theories seize on the militia clause of the Amendment as qualifying, rather than amplifying, the enumerated right. Scholars adopting collective readings stress that the Amendment was essentially adopted in an effort to protect the state militias from being destroyed by a powerful and potentially tyrannical federal government. The means chosen to protect a state's ability to field a militia was to ensure that the public could be armed for that purpose, but that purpose only. Followed to its logical conclusion, this reading renders the Amendment largely irrelevant in modern American society, as the general militia has fallen into disuse.

*The Individual Rights Interpretation (The Standard Model): The Basics* Proponents of this model argue that the plain language and structure of the Second Amendment, the Framers' understanding of the right to keep and bear arms, as well as the understanding of the right to keep and bear arms during the Reconstruction Era, all indicate that it was meant to protect an individual's right to keep and bear arms, independent of militia service.

On the most fundamental level, commentators arguing for an individual rights interpretation point to the plain language of the Second Amendment. First, scholars point out that the eighteenth century meaning of the term "militia" included all citizens who qualified for military service, as opposed to organized military units like the modern National Guard. Indeed, this general, unorganized militia is still provided for by federal law today. Therefore, a reading that interprets the militia clause of the Second Amendment as limiting the right to keep and bear arms to individuals participating in modern, organized military units, such as the National Guard, is historically inaccurate.

*Individual Rights: "The People" in the Amendments and Framing-Era History* In addition, proponents of the individual rights reading point to the undeniable fact that the right enumerated in the Second Amendment is conferred upon "the people," as opposed to the states or organized militia units. Stressing consistency in construing the Constitution, these commentators argue that "the people" referred to in the Second Amendment are the same people referred to in the First, Fourth, Ninth, and Tenth Amendments, namely individuals. Furthermore, these commentators point out that the Framers knew how to articulate the difference between "the states" and "the people," as the two terms are used to describe different entities in the Tenth Amendment. Indeed, this reading of "the people" is not a new concept. For example, abolitionist Frederick Douglass argued against limited readings of the term "the people," which contributed to the constitutional survival of slavery. Mr. Douglass questioned interpretations that substituted a part of the people for the whole people. He wrote that such selective readings of the term disregarded "the plain and commonsense reading of the instrument itself; by showing that the Constitution does not mean what it says, and says what it does not mean."

Scholars adopting an individual rights reading of the Second Amendment also rely on framing-era history to support their interpretation. This historical analysis often begins with an examination of the English right to arms, from which the American Second Amendment descended. To this end, William Blackstone's *Commentaries on the Laws of England*, are often used to provide perspective on the Framers' understanding of the English right to arms. Undoubtedly, Blackstone's writings greatly influenced eighteenth century American political thought. Blackstone described the English right to arms as an "auxiliary" right that was necessary in order for subjects "to protect and maintain inviolate the three great and primary rights, of *personal* security, *personal* liberty, and *private* property." Indeed, it is hard to understand how a government-controlled, collective right to arms would serve the purpose of protecting the English triumvirate, which were *personal* and *private* rights. As the ideas embodied in this personal "auxiliary" right evolved into the Second Amendment, the language qualifying the right to arms in the English Declaration of Rights was eliminated.

*The Circumstances Surrounding the Second Amendment's Passage* With this English history in mind, individual rights theorists focus on the circumstances surrounding ratification of the Bill of Rights in order to understand the Second Amendment. This focus stresses that the Second Amendment developed out of a concern that the newly ratified Constitution, which gave Congress the ability to raise and support a standing army and also ceded extensive control over the militia to the federal government, significantly increased the possibility of tyrannical rule by creating a potential monopoly on the use of force. The concern being that Congress could create such a monopoly by "rais[ing] and support[ing] Armies," while failing to "provide for organizing, arming, and disciplining, the Militia." The Second Amendment sought to counter this monopoly of force, not by reapportioning power over the militia to the states, but by reinforcing the idea that the *people themselves* could not be disarmed. Therefore, with regard to the balance of power in American society, the future of the militia became largely irrelevant "because the people's right to have weapons was to be sacrosanct." Indeed, modern case law supports the assertion that Congress's Article I power over the organized state militias, in the form of the National Guard, is plenary and is not restrained by the Second Amendment. Under this interpretation, the militia clause of the Second Amendment merely expressed a preference for the use of a general militia over a standing army or select militia, and encouraged "the federal government to keep the militia in good order."

This individualized interpretation of the right to keep and bear arms also seemed to predominate over seventy years after the Second Amendment was ratified during America's next big constitutional moment: the drafting and ratification of the Fourteenth Amendment. The consequences of adopting an individual rights interpretation of the Second Amendment will be the focus of the remainder of this comment, but first it is necessary to examine the Supreme Court's most direct treatment of the Amendment.

## Direct Treatment of the Second Amendment by the U.S. Supreme Court: *United States v. Miller*

The Supreme Court has contributed little in the way of resolving the Second Amendment debate. In *United States v. Miller*, the Court's most direct treatment of the Second Amendment, has been described as a "lazy and ambiguous 1939 opinion from which almost nothing—or almost anything—could be inferred." [Nelson Lund, *Outsider Voices on Guns and the Constitution*, Constitutional Commentary, 2000.] However, it has also been suggested that *Miller* is so frustrating to both sides of the partisan debate over the Second Amendment precisely because it comes down in the middle ground between the two extremes.

In *Miller*, the District Court for the Western District of Arkansas sustained a demurrer and quashed an indictment of Jack Miller and Frank Layton. The indictment charged Miller and Layton with transporting an unregistered firearm (a shotgun having a barrel of less than 18-inches) across state lines without a stamp-affixed written order, in violation of the National Firearms Act of 1934. The defendants' demurrer alleged, in part, that the National Firearms Act violated the Second Amendment. The district court sustained the demurrer and quashed the indictment, holding that section 11 of the Act violated the Second Amendment. The Supreme Court heard the case on direct appeal and reasoned that the purpose of the Second Amendment was to assure the continued existence and effectiveness of the militia. The Court held:

> In absence of any evidence tending to show that the possession or use of a "shotgun having a barrel of less than eighteen inches in length" at this time has some reasonable relationship to the preservation or efficiency of a well regulated militia, we cannot say that the Second Amendment guarantees the right to keep and bear such an instrument. Certainly it is not within judicial notice that this weapon is any part of the ordinary military equipment or that its use could contribute to the common defense.

The Court was forced to rely on judicial notice due to the fact that the defendant-appellees did not appear on appeal. In its holding, the Court linked the right to arms to the preservation or efficiency of a well regulated militia by requiring that arms have some utility for militia service in order to fall under the Amendment's protection. However, the Court did not make this connection in the sense promoted by the collective rights theory. The collective rights theories tether the right to keep and bear arms to *an individual's* participation in the militia. However, in *Miller* the Court connects the right to keep and bear arms to *the weapon's* utility for militia service. At the very least, *Miller's* arms-based approach suggests that individuals have a right to keep add bear arms "having some reasonable relationship to the preservation or efficiency of a well regulated militia."

## Constitutional Rationales for the Individual Right to Keep and Bear Arms

With this background in place, it is possible to begin examining the consequences of recognizing an individual's right to keep and bear arms, unrelated to service in an organized militia. Certainly, recognizing such a right does not end the inquiry, but merely provides a reason to begin developing a framework for determining whether specific gun control legislation or disarmament treaties infringe upon the right. The first step in such an endeavor is to articulate the constitutional rationales for the individual right guaranteed by the Second Amendment. . . .

*The Military Function* Military readiness is sometimes purported to be a rationale for the Second Amendment that should be considered in constructing any logical Second Amendment analytical framework. This interpretation follows logically from the *Miller* decision, as the Court seemed to indicate that arms with military utility would be subject to some protection. However, this argument illustrates the principal flaw in *Miller* and the militia-centric readings of the Second Amendment. Although historically the militia was held in high regard as a military fighting force, military readiness, in the form of a well-armed and organized citizen militia to be tapped for military duty during times of war, was arguably not an important purpose of drafting the Second Amendment. Article I had already provided Congress "with virtually plenary powers to organize, train, and maintain a military establishment as efficient and powerful as it can afford." The Article I powers also seemed to provide for organized, state-based military units. Furthermore, the federal government was given the power to use the Militia to "execute the Laws of the Union, suppress Insurrections and repel Invasions." Therefore, defense of the nation, and control of the forces necessary to provide that defense, was largely turned over to the Congress in Article I. The Second Amendment did not attempt to reapportion that military power. . . .

*The Self-Preservation Function* This comment is not arguing that there was not sentiment among the Framers that the general militia was still the best military model for defense of the nation. However, this comment is arguing that even if this was the case, the powers granted to Congress in Article I indicate that the Framers had chosen a different military model—a federally controlled army and select militia. Indeed, post-ratification sources discussing the continued utility of the militia speak in terms of repelling "sudden invasions, domestic insurrections, and domestic usurpations of power by rulers," [Stephen P. Halbrook, *That Every Man Be Armed: The Evolution of a Constitutional Right*, 1984] as opposed to wartime use of the militia as an effective fighting force. In this sense, the continued utility of the general militia, in the form of private citizens keeping and bearing private arms, was to provide a means for collective self-defense in emergencies where, for some reason, governmentally controlled forces could not provide an adequate defense. Examples of such situations are "sudden invasions" and "domestic insurrections."

In addition, the Framers believed that an armed citizenry would serve an internal checking function designed to prevent the government from using the standing armies and select militias, which Article I made a reality, to oppress the private citizenry. In light of the fear that federal power over the military engendered among the Framers, the Second Amendment makes the most sense when viewed not as a means for the people to prepare for military service, but as an effective counterbalance to the federal government's military power. Supreme Court Justice Joseph Story, succinctly described this internal checking function. He stated:

> It is against sound policy for a free people to keep up large military establishments and standing armies in time of peace, both from the enormous expenses, with which they are attended, and the facile means, which they afford to ambitious and unprincipled rulers, to subvert the government, or trample upon the rights of the people. *The right of the citizens to keep and bear arms has justly been considered, as the palladium of the liberties of the republic; since it offers a strong moral check against usurpation and arbitrary power of the rulers*; and will generally, even if these are successful in the first instance, enable the people to resist and triumph over them [emphasis added].

Thus, the individual right to keep and bear arms was meant, in part, to serve the self-preservation function by preserving the means for citizens to perform acts of collective self-defense.

Perhaps the most uncontroversial purpose of the individual right enumerated in the Second Amendment was to ensure that the people would not be deprived the means to pursue their personal right of self-defense. Although this assertion may seem incongruent given the absence of any mention of personal self-defense in the Amendment's text, the preeminence of the right of self-defense in English common law, in liberal theory, which played an important role in shaping political thought in the colonies, and in the realities of life at the time of the framing, all indicate that the most plausible reason for such silence is that the right to use private arms for personal self-defense was simply taken for granted by the Framers. In short, the right to self-defense was understood as an unenumerated, natural right reserved to the people, which could be lawfully exercised when society was unable to protect the individual. Modern case law upholding and enforcing statutes that immunize police from suits for negligent failure to prevent the commissioning of crimes, and holding that "a government and its agents are under no general duty to provide public services, such as police protection, to any particular individual citizen" are modern reminders that society is not always able to protect individuals from harm. Thus, an individual's right to keep and bear arms was also meant to serve the self-preservation function by preserving the means for citizens to perform acts of personal self-defense.

*The Moral Function* Finally, a moral function has been associated with the Second Amendment. This function is directly tied to the republican ideal that being armed was "essential to the development of civic virtue and good moral character." This rationale is built on the idea that the responsibility and self-discipline associated with owning firearms and developing proficiency in the use of firearms contributes to building a citizenry of republican virtue. However, this rational also works in reverse. In order to build such civic virtue, firearms ownership must be limited to the virtuous citizenry. This function will be referred to as the "moral function."

With these three functions in mind, one is able to develop a functional framework for Second Amendment review of gun control legislation. . . .

## Implications of the Individual Rights Framework

The major implication of adopting the individual rights theory of the Second Amendment, and the analytical framework proposed in this comment, is that bans on the private ownership of protected firearms carry a strong presumption of invalidity. As a result, any international treaty proscribing the sale of small arms to the American civilian population would likely be in direct conflict with the Second Amendment. In addition, the adoption of the ban-based gun control policies, currently employed in many foreign democracies, such as Japan and Great Britain, would also run headlong into the Second Amendment.

However, borrowing licensing and permit-based policies are not foreclosed by adopting an individual rights reading of the Second Amendment. So long as these policies ensure that licensing and permitting schemes would (1) only be instituted to serve important governmental purposes, (2) provide clear standards for issuing licenses leaving little discretion to the issuing authority, and (3) provide sufficient procedural safeguards, then borrowing would not necessarily conflict with the Second Amendment. In addition, policy makers and academics intent on borrowing from other countries should also look to countries, such as Switzerland, that manage to have widespread private ownership of firearms, while maintaining low violent crime rates.

The unique relationship between firearms and the American citizen has been attributed to a number of factors including armed conflict between American settlers and American Indians, the role of the citizen militia in creating the republic, and vigilantism on the Western frontier. Although there are cultural similarities between the United States and nations like Canada and Australia, which also emerged from the British Commonwealth, there are also important differences that help explain the unique role of armed civilians in the American constitutional scheme. First, unlike both Canada and Australia, the United States was born in a violent, armed assertion of its national independence. In addition, unlike their Canadian and Australian counterparts, early Americans pushed West into a violent frontier before there was any semblance of government protection. Americans settling the Western frontier relied on private arms as their sole means of protection. Conversely, the North-West Mounted Police and centrally controlled Australian police provided state sanctioned security for settlers of the frontiers in Canada and Australia, respectively. In addition, the fighting between Australian and Canadian settlers and the indigenous populations of those countries was much less fierce and short lived when compared to the American experience.

This background explains why the right to keep and bear arms plays such an important role in American society and is prominently displayed in the Bill of Rights. However, in the end, whether the right is viewed as embarrassing, terrifying, or as an essential means to individual liberty and personal autonomy, the fact of the right's existence remains. Moving forward, energy would be best spent developing a framework to delineate the contours of the individual right enumerated in the Second Amendment, rather then [sic] straining to deny its existence. It is only through squarely and honestly facing the Second Amendment, and the right it enumerates, that society can start to work towards sane domestic and international gun control policies. Otherwise, society will continue to make the fatal mistake of running from a lion in the bush.

# Are Gun Manufacturers Liable for Negligence?

# Chapter Preface

## Case Overview: *Hamilton v. Beretta* (2001)

The first incarnation of the *Hamilton v. Beretta* case began in January 1995, in the U.S. District Court for the Eastern District of New York, where numerous plaintiffs sued forty-nine gun manufacturers for negligent marketing, design defect, ultra-hazardous activity, and fraud. The plaintiffs were all relatives of people killed by handguns. The district court threw out the claims of product liability and fraud but allowed the case to continue on the negligent marketing cause. The case went to trial in 1999, by which time there were twenty-five defendants and seven plaintiffs, the latter including the addition of a living victim, Stephen Fox, who had been permanently disabled after being shot with a gun purportedly purchased out of the trunk of a car.

Plaintiffs argued that the gun manufacturers marketed and distributed their handguns negligently, inundating the underground markets of southern states—which have weaker gun control laws—with guns subsequently purchased by minors and criminals, guns that eventually made their way north, contributing to a sizable illegal market for guns in the New York area.

Only one gun was recovered from the death scenes of the plaintiffs' relatives, making it impossible for the plaintiffs to determine which gun manufacturers' weapons had been used, so the district court allowed the plaintiffs to argue on the theory of market share liability. The trial lasted four weeks, concluding with the jury handing down a special verdict: they determined that fifteen of the twenty-five defendants had not used reasonable care in distributing their guns and that nine of those fifteen had proximately caused two deaths. In these cases, no damages were awarded, but in the case of living victim Stephen Fox, the jury awarded damages against three defendants to Fox and his mother, determining the proportion of liability and damages on the basis of national market share.

The court denied the defendants' motion for judgment, delineating several opinions on how the defendants were able to reasonably take better care in their distribution and marketing practices; the court determined that gun manufacturers, like other manufacturers, were able to foresee and protect against certain risks, which created a "protective relationship" between them and potential gun victims.

The defendants appealed to the Second Circuit of the U.S. Court of Appeals, which certified to the New York Court of Appeals two questions: (1) Was it the defendants' duty to the plaintiffs to exercise reasonable care in marketing and distributing the defendants' handguns, and (2) Could liability in this case be based on market share?

Yes, the plaintiffs asserted. The defendants, they argued, had a degree of control over the marketing and distribution and knew that large numbers of their guns were being used in crime and entering the illegal market, and these factors, coupled with New York's strict gun control policies and the inherently lethal nature of the manufacturers' products, led to a duty to exercise care on the part of the defendants. The defendants, in response, continued to argue that they could not be held responsible for the behavior and acts of third parties over which they had no control and that if any changes *were* to be made in the practices of gun sales and distribution, they should happen through legislative and regulatory channels, not through the courts.

The court in this case agreed with the defendants. For one, it found that "foreseeability, alone, does not define duty" and that plaintiffs were required to show not only that the defendants owed a general duty to society, but also that they owed a specific duty to the plaintiffs themselves. The court found that the defendants did not. Otherwise, the court determined, potential defendants could be subjected "to limitless liability to an indeterminate class of persons conceivably injured by any negligence." The judges ruled that they could not extend to the defendants the duty to control the actions of others—that is, those who may have sold the guns illegally or used them in crimes. There was no direct relationship in these cases between the defendants and the plaintiffs, the court ruled. Furthermore, the court found that market share liability was inappropriate in a case such as this, in which the products that cause death, if found, could be individually and specifically identified and differentiated, as to make and manufacturer. Market share liability is only appropriate, they explained, when it is impossible to prove which manufacturer created the product that caused the injury, such as in the case of fungible drugs; inability to recover the guns used in the crimes did not "justify the extraordinary step of applying market share liability," particularly given, the court wrote, that the defendants' practices may have varied widely.

Four years later, Congress passed the controversial Protection of Lawful Commerce in Arms Act, shielding arms manufacturers and retailers from such liability suits, except for when the products are defective or when breach of contract or criminal misconduct on the part of the manufacturer or retailer is involved.

"*Foreseeability, alone, does not define duty—it merely determines the scope of the duty once it is determined to exist.*"

# The Court's Decision: Handgun Manufacturers Are Not Liable

*Judge Richard C. Wesley*

*New York native Richard C. Wesley received his JD from Cornell Law School in 1974. He worked in private practice until 1986 and during that time was elected twice to the New York State Assembly. Subsequently, he was elected as a justice of the Seventh Judicial District of the New York Supreme Court, a position he held for fourteen years; from 1991 to 1994, he was supervising judge of the criminal courts. Governor Mario Cuomo appointed him to New York's Supreme Court Appellate Division in 1994; Governor George Pataki made him associate judge of the New York Court of Appeals in 1997; and President George W. Bush nominated Wesley to the Second Circuit of the U.S. Court of Appeals in 2003.*

*Handing down the New York Court of Appeals's opinion in* Hamilton v. Beretta, *Judge Richard C. Wesley and his fellow judges found that the relationship between the plaintiffs and defendants in this case—the plaintiffs being gunshot victims and family members of deceased gunshot victims, and the defendants being gun manufacturers—did not create for the defendants a duty to protect the plaintiffs. The court did not accept the*

Judge Richard C. Wesley, majority opinion, *Hamilton v. Beretta*, Court of Appeals of New York, April 26, 2001.

*plaintiffs' argument that the defendants held a duty of care under the negligent entrustment doctrine and found that market share liability, which apportions blame according to a defendant's particular share of the industry, did not apply to the circumstances of this case.*

The threshold question in any negligence action is: does defendant owe a legally recognized duty of care to plaintiff? Courts traditionally "fix the duty point by balancing factors, including the reasonable expectations of parties and society generally, the proliferation of claims, the likelihood of unlimited or insurer-like liability, disproportionate risk and reparation allocation, and public policies affecting the expansion or limitation of new channels of liability." Thus, in determining whether a duty exists, "courts must be mindful of the precedential, and consequential, future effects of their rulings, and 'limit the legal consequences of wrongs to a controllable degree.'"

Foreseeability, alone, does not define duty—it merely determines the scope of the duty once it is determined to exist. The injured party must show that a defendant owed not merely a general duty to society but a specific duty to him or her, for "[w]ithout a duty running directly to the injured person there can be no liability in damages, however careless the conduct or foreseeable the harm." That is required in order to avoid subjecting an actor "to limitless liability to an indeterminate class of persons conceivably injured by any negligence in that act." Moreover, any extension of the scope of duty must be tailored to reflect accurately the extent that its social benefits outweigh its costs.

The District Court imposed a duty on gun manufacturers "to take reasonable steps available at the point of sale to primary distributors to reduce the possibility that these instruments will fall into the hands of those likely to misuse them." We have been cautious, however, in extending liability to defendants for their failure to control the conduct of others. "A defendant generally has no duty to control the conduct of third persons so as to prevent them from harming others, even where as a practical matter defendant can exercise such control." This judicial resistance to the expansion of duty grows out of practical concerns both about potentially limitless liability and about the unfairness of imposing liability for the acts of another.

## Relationships That May Create Duty

A duty may arise, however, where there is a relationship either between defendant and a third-person tortfeasor that encompasses defendant's actual control of the third person's actions, or between defendant and plaintiff that requires defendant to protect plaintiff from the conduct of others. Examples of these relationships include master and servant, parent and child, and common carriers and their passengers.

The key in each is that the defendant's relationship with either the tortfeasor or the plaintiff places the defendant in the best position to protect against the risk of harm. In addition, the specter of limitless liability is not present because the class of potential plaintiffs to whom the duty is owed is circumscribed by the relationship. We have, for instance, recognized that landowners have a duty to protect tenants, patrons or invitees from foreseeable harm caused by the criminal conduct of others while they are on the premises. However, this duty does not extend beyond that limited class of plaintiffs to members of the community at large. In *Waters* [*v. New York City Hous. Auth.*], for example, we held that the owner of a housing project who failed to keep the building's door locks in good repair did not owe a duty to a passerby to protect her from being dragged off the street into the building and assaulted. The Court concluded that imposing such a duty on landowners would do little to minimize crime, and the social benefits to be gained did "not warrant the extension of the landowner's duty to maintain secure premises to the millions of individuals who use the sidewalks of New York City each day and are thereby exposed to the dangers of street crime."

A similar rationale is relevant here. The pool of possible plaintiffs is very large—potentially, any of the thousands of victims of gun violence. Further, the connection between defendants, the criminal wrongdoers and plaintiffs is remote, running through several links in a chain consisting of at least the manufacturer, the federally licensed distributor or wholesaler, and the first retailer. The chain most often includes numerous subsequent legal purchasers or even a thief. Such broad liability, potentially encompassing all gunshot crime victims, should not be imposed without a more tangible showing that the defendants were a direct link in the causal chain that resulted in the plaintiffs' injuries, and that the defendants were realistically in a position to prevent the wrongs. Giving plaintiffs' evidence the benefit of every favorable inference, they have not shown that the gun used to harm plaintiff Fox came from a source amenable to the exercise of any duty of care that plaintiffs would impose upon defendant manufacturers.

## Foreseeability

Plaintiffs make two alternative arguments in support of a duty determination here. The first arises from a manufacturer's "special ability to detect and guard against the risks associated with [its] products [and] warrants placing all manufacturers, including these defendants, in a *protective relationship with those foreseeably and potentially put in harm's way by their products*" [emphasis added]. Plaintiffs predicate the existence of this protective duty—particularly when lethal or hazardous products are involved—on foreseeability of harm and our products liability cases such as *MacPherson v Buick Motor Co.*

As we noted earlier, a duty and the corresponding liability it imposes do *not* rise from mere foreseeability of the harm. Moreover, none of plaintiffs' proof demonstrated that a change in marketing techniques would likely have prevented their injuries. Indeed, plaintiffs did not present any evidence tending to show to what degree their risk of injury was enhanced by the presence of negligently marketed and distributed guns, as opposed to the risk presented by all guns in society.

The cases involving the distribution or handling of hazardous materials, relied upon by plaintiffs, do not support the imposition of a duty of care in marketing handguns. The manufacturer's duty in each case was based either on a products liability theory—that is, the product was defective because of the failure to include a safety feature—or on a failure to warn.

Certainly too, a manufacturer may be held liable for complicity in dangerous or illegal activity. Here, defendants' products are concededly not defective—if anything, the problem is that they work too well. Nor have plaintiffs asserted a defective warnings claim or presented sufficient evidence to demonstrate that defendants could have taken reasonable steps that would have prevented their injuries. Likewise, this case can hardly be analogized to those in which a duty has been imposed upon owners or possessors of hazardous substances to safeguard against unsupervised access by children.

## The Manufacturer's General Duty of Care

Plaintiffs' also assert that a general duty of care arises out of the gun manufacturers' ability to reduce the risk of illegal gun trafficking through control of the marketing and distribution of their products. The District Court accepted this proposition and posited a series of structural changes in defendants' marketing and distribution regimes that might "reduce the risk of criminal misuse by insuring that the first sale was by a responsible merchant to a responsible buyer." Those changes, and others proposed by plaintiffs that a jury might reasonably find subsumed in a gun manufacturer's duty of care, would have the unavoidable effect of eliminating a significant number of lawful sales to "responsible" buyers by "responsible" Federal firearms licensees (FFLs) who would be cut out of the distribution chain under the suggested "reforms." Plaintiffs, however, presented no evidence, either through the testimony of experts or the submission of authoritative reports, showing any statistically significant relationship between *particular classes* of dealers and crime guns. To impose a general duty of care upon the makers of firearms under these circumstances because of their purported ability to control marketing and distribution of their products would conflict with the principle that any judicial recognition of a duty of care must be based upon an assessment of its efficacy in promoting a social benefit as against its costs and burdens. Here, imposing such a general duty of care would create not only an indeterminate class of plaintiffs but also an indeterminate class of defendants whose liability might have little relationship to the benefits of controlling illegal guns.

## The Negligent Entrustment Doctrine

Finally, plaintiffs and the District Court identify an alternative basis for imposing a duty of care here under the negligent entrustment doctrine, arising out of the firearms manufacturers' authority over "downstream distributors and retailers" to whom their products are delivered. The owner or possessor of a dangerous instrument is under a duty to entrust it to a responsible person whose use does not create an unreasonable risk of harm to others. The duty may extend through successive, reasonably anticipated entrustees. There are, however, fatal impediments to imposing a general duty of care here under a negligent entrustment theory.

The tort of negligent entrustment is based on the degree of knowledge the supplier of a chattel has or should have concerning the entrustee's propensity to use the chattel in an improper or dangerous fashion. Gun sales have subjected suppliers to liability under this theory. Of course, without the requisite knowledge, the tort of negligent entrustment does not lie.

The negligent entrustment doctrine might well support the extension of a duty to manufacturers to avoid selling to certain distributors in circumstances where the manufacturer knows or has reason to know those distributors are engaging in substantial sales of guns into the gun-trafficking market on a consistent basis. Here, however, plaintiffs did not present such evidence. Instead, they claimed that manufacturers should not engage in certain broad categories of sales. Once again, plaintiffs' duty calculation comes up short. General statements about an industry are not the stuff by which a common-law court fixes the duty point. Without a showing that specific groups of dealers play a disproportionate role in supplying the illegal gun market, the sweep of plaintiffs' duty theory is far wider than the danger it seeks to avert.

## The Tracing of Guns Used in Crimes

At trial, plaintiffs' experts did surmise that since manufacturers receive crime gun trace requests conducted by the Bureau of Alcohol, Tobacco and Firearms (BATF), they could analyze those requests to locate retailers who disproportionately served as crime gun sources, and cut off distributors who do business with them. In essence, plaintiffs argue that defendants had an affirmative duty to investigate and identify corrupt dealers. This is neither feasible nor appropriate for the manufacturers.

Plaintiffs' experts explained that a crime gun trace is the means by which the BATF reconstructs the distribution history of a gun used in a crime or recovered by the police. While manufacturers may be generally aware of traces for which they are contacted, they are not told the purpose of the trace, nor are they informed of the results. The BATF does not disclose any subsequently acquired retailer or purchaser information to the manufacturer. Moreover, manufacturers are not in a position to acquire such information on their own. Indeed, plaintiffs' law enforcement experts agreed that manufacturers should not make any attempt to investigate illegal gun trafficking on their own since such attempts could disrupt pending criminal investigations and endanger the lives of undercover officers.

## The Defendants Did Not Owe the Plaintiffs the Duty Claimed

Federal law already has implemented a statutory and regulatory scheme to ensure seller "responsibility" through licensing requirements and buyer "responsibility" through background checks. While common-law principles can supplement a manufacturer's statutory duties, we should be cautious in imposing novel theories of tort liability while the difficult problem of illegal gun sales in the United States remains the focus of a national policy debate.

In sum, analysis of this State's longstanding precedents demonstrates that defendants—given the evidence presented here—did not owe plaintiffs the duty they claim; we therefore answer the first certified question in the negative.

## Market Share Liability: Background

The Second Circuit has asked us also to determine if our market share liability jurisprudence is applicable to this case. Having concluded that these defendant-manufacturers did not owe the claimed duty to these plaintiffs, we arguably need not reach the market share issue. However, because of its particularly significant role in this case, it seems prudent to answer the second question.

Market share liability provides an exception to the general rule that in common-law negligence actions, a plaintiff must prove that the defendant's conduct was a cause-in-fact of the injury. This Court first examined and adopted the market share theory of liability in *Hymowitz v. Eli Lilly & Co.* In *Hy-mowitz*, we held that plaintiffs injured by the drug DES were not required to prove which defendant manufactured the drug that injured them but instead, every manufacturer would be held responsible for every plaintiff's injury based on its share of the DES market. Market share liability was necessary in *Hy-mowitz* because DES was a fungible product and identification of the actual manufacturer that caused the injury to a particular plaintiff was impossible. The Court carefully noted that the DES situation was unique. Key to our decision were the facts that (1) the manufacturers acted in a parallel manner to produce an identical, generically marketed product; (2) the manifestations of injury were far removed from the time of ingestion of the product; and (3) the Legislature made a clear policy decision to revive these time-barred DES claims.

## The Differences Between This Case and Previous Market Share Liability Cases

Circumstances here are markedly different. Unlike DES, guns are not identical, fungible products. Significantly, it is often possible to identify the caliber and manufacturer of the handgun that caused injury to a particular plaintiff. Even more importantly—given the negligent marketing theory on which plaintiffs tried this cases—plaintiffs have never asserted that the manufacturers' marketing techniques were uniform. Each manufacturer engaged in different marketing activities that allegedly contributed to the illegal handgun market in different ways and to different extents. Plaintiffs made no attempt to establish the relative fault of each manufacturer, but instead sought to hold them all liable based simply on market share.

In *Hymowitz*, each manufacturer engaged in tortious conduct parallel to that of all other manufacturers, creating the same risk to the public at large by manufacturing the same defective product. Market share was an accurate reflection of the risk they posed. Here, the distribution and sale of every gun is not equally negligent, nor does it involve a defective product. Defendants engaged in widely-varied conduct creating varied risks. Thus, a manufacturer's share of the national handgun market does not necessarily correspond to the amount of risk created by its alleged tortious conduct. No case has applied the market share theory of liability to such varied conduct and wisely so.

We recognize the difficulty in proving precisely which manufacturer caused any particular plaintiff's injuries since crime guns are often not recovered. Inability to locate evidence, however, does not alone justify the extraordinary step of applying market share liability. Rather, a more compelling policy reason—as was shown in the DES cases—is required for the imposition of market share liability.

Notably, courts in New York and other jurisdictions have refused to extend the market share theory where products were not fungible and differing degrees of risk were created. Similarly, plaintiffs here have not shown a set of compelling circumstances akin to those in *Hymowitz* justifying a departure from traditional common-law principles of causation.

## The Court's Final Decision

This case challenges us to rethink traditional notions of duty, liability and causation. Tort law is ever changing; it is a reflection of the complexity and vitality of daily life. Although plaintiffs have presented us with a novel theory—negligent marketing of a potentially lethal yet legal product, based upon the acts not of one manufacturer, but of an industry—we are unconvinced that, on the record before us, the duty plaintiffs wish to impose is either reasonable or circumscribed. Nor does the market share theory of liability accurately measure defendants' conduct. Whether, in a different case, a duty may arise remains a question for the future.

Accordingly, both certified questions should be answered in the negative.

Following certification of questions by the United States Court of Appeals for the Second Circuit and acceptance of the questions by this Court pursuant to section 500.17 of the Rules of Practice of the New York State Court of Appeals, and after hearing argument by counsel for the parties and consideration of the briefs and the record submitted, certified questions answered in the negative. Opinion by Judge Wesley. Chief Judge Kaye and Judges Smith, Levine, Ciparick, Rosenblatt and Graffeo concur.

> *"Plaintiffs are ... required to make a strong showing of a causal link before a duty and corresponding liability would be imposed upon defendant gun manufacturers."*

# The Significance of the Suits Against Gun Makers

## *Daniel M. Duval, et al.*

*This commentary was written in 2001 by a group of then-students of Cornell Law School, Daniel M. Duval, Timothy Q. Edwards, Edward K. Halperin, Ingrid A. Holewinski, Alethea K. Rebman, and Tanya Waldrop.*

*Here the authors summarize the conclusions of the court in the* Hamilton *case and the effects on subsequent law. Additionally, they present unanswered questions raised by the court's decisions and written reasons for those decisions. Finally, they examine the similar and dissimilar decisions reached in other jurisdictions.*

## The State of the Law Before *Hamilton*

In general, in determining whether a legally recognized duty of care exists, New York courts have traditionally relied upon an analysis of a number of balancing factors, including, but not limited to, the forseeability of risk and the existence of a specific duty of care owed to the injured party. Essential to the finding of a duty of care has been the defendant's abil-

Daniel M. Duval, Timonthy Q. Edwards, Edward K. Halperin, Ingrid A. Holewinski, Alethea K. Rebman, and Tanya Waldrop, "Commentary for Case Overview: Hamilton v. Beretta, Court of Appeals of New York," *Legal Information Institute*, 2001. Reproduced by permission.

ity to protect against the risk of harm, with liability extending only to those defendants "in the best position" to prevent the injuries of a limited, specific class. Thus, the Court of Appeals has been reluctant to impose liability for the acts of another without a specific relationship between the parties, such as parent/child or master/servant, and has sought to avoid placing defendants in situations of unlimited liability based upon third-party conduct.

Decisions have not always been consistent, however, in holding that "unending liability" is reason enough to limit the scope of duty. *See e.g. MacPherson v. Buick Motor Co.; Millington v. S.E. Elevator Co.* Moreover, in some circumstances, the doctrine of negligent entrustment has dictated that control of a dangerous instrument imposes a duty to entrust it to a responsible person whose use does not create an unreasonable risk of harm to others. Restatement (Second) of Torts § 390; *but see Earsing v. Nelson* (holding that the theory of negligent entrustment does not extend to the manufacturer of an air gun). In general, the Court has avoided enlarging the scope of duty unless public policy goals would be furthered and the benefits to society would outweigh the costs of imposing a new duty of care upon a large number of potential defendants. *See, e.g., Waters v. New York City Hous. Auth.*

Market-share liability has been a theory of recovery in the New York courts for plaintiffs harmed by a fungible product whose manufacturer was impossible to determine, and where the manufacturers generically marketed their product. *See Hymowitz v. Eli Lily & Co.* In instances where market-share liability has been applied, the defendant tortfeasors' liability has been apportioned among all manufacturers based upon the market share of each at the time of the tortuous act. In New York as well as other jurisdictions, market-share liability has never applied where products were not fungible, nor where each independent manufacturer's conduct created different degrees of harm. *See e.g. Brenner v. American Cyanamid Co.*

## The Effect of *Hamilton* on Current Law: Duty of Care

The Court of Appeals held that Defendant handgun manufacturers do not owe Plaintiffs a duty to exercise reasonable care in the marketing and distribution of their product, and that, if liability were to exist in this case, it would not be apportionable on a market-share basis.

The holding in *Hamilton* thus limits the duty of care and consequent liability that may be imposed upon a gun manufacturer where the negligence alleged is based upon the acts of the gun industry rather than the acts of one manufacturer. The Court found the relationship between the gun manufacturers, the criminal wrongdoers, and Plaintiffs to be too remote to create a duty of care. The Court stated that such a duty should not be imposed without a more "tangible showing" of a direct causal link to the injuries and a showing that Defendants were "realistically in a position to prevent the wrongs." This suggests that even with the benefit of favorable inferences, plaintiffs are still required to make a strong showing of a causal link before a duty and corresponding liability would be imposed upon defendant gun manufacturers.

In addition, the Court limited the relevance of the foreseeability of harm as a determinative factor in establishing a duty of care, and likewise distinguished and thus curtailed the applicability of theories of products liability exemplified in cases such as *MacPherson v. Buick Motor Co.* In *Hamilton*, the Court found no showing of a product defect or failure to warn, and refused to analogize the relationship between the gun manufacturers and Plaintiffs to the protective relationship existing in other industries, thus eliminating the potential for such reasoning to succeed in future challenges to the gun industry.

The Court further held that a duty of care cannot be imposed based upon the negligent entrustment doctrine because Plaintiffs did not show that Defendants knew or had reason to know that the distributors sold guns into the illegal gun-trafficking market on a consistent basis. The Court suggested that such a duty might be imposed if the manufacturer had the requisite knowledge that specific groups of dealers played a "disproportionate role in supplying the illegal gun market." The Court's extension of duty in these instances might be further limited, however, by the Court's refusal to acknowledge an affirmative duty on the part of manufacturers to identify and investigate corrupt dealers.

## Market Share Liability

In finding that liability in this case may not be apportioned on a market-share basis, the Court concluded that guns were not identical, fungible products, and in this respect, differed from the situation in *Hymowitz v. Eli Lilly & Co.*, where the Court applied market share liability with respect to the birth control drug DES. In addition, the Court found that although Plaintiff sought to hold all Defendants liable based on market share, the manufacturers' marketing techniques were not uniform, and no attempt was made to determine relative fault. A further obstacle Plaintiffs failed to overcome was the fact that a differing degree of risk for abuse was created based on Defendants' varying conduct, and that such risk should be assessed in light of the additional probability that Plaintiffs' injuries were caused from non-negligently marketed guns. Thus, even if Defendants' market share in the negligently marketed gun market could be determined, it seems the liability would further be reduced by the probability that a negligently marketed gun in fact caused the injuries *See* Twerksi & Sebok, *Liability Without Cause? Further Ruminations on Cause-in-Fact as Applied to Handgun Liability.* This suggests that the ultimate liability imposed if market-share theory were applied might be more difficult to determine than the District Court's calculations indicate and would result in far less liability overall for specific manufacturers.

## Unanswered Questions

The Court based its finding in part on the lack of evidence directly placing the Defendant in the causal chain of events leading to the Plaintiff's injuries. If stronger evidence were presented that the manufacturer negligently marketed its handguns and proximately caused Plaintiffs' injuries, could the manufacturer have owed a duty of reasonable care to the victims of handgun shootings? What kind of evidence, if any, could ever demonstrate that negligence?

The Court noted that the negligent entrustment doctrine might support the extension of a duty to manufacturers to avoid selling to certain distributors in circumstances where the manufacturer knows or has reason to know that those distributors are engaging in substantial sales of guns into the illegal gun-trafficking market on a consistent basis. What constitutes "substantial sales" into the illegal gun-trafficking market?

Would the difficulty in the market-share liability calculations cited in the Court's opinion, limiting damages to the proportion to which defendant's negligent marketing enhanced the risk of injury by handguns, lead the Court to be less likely to apply market-share liability in the future?

## Survey of the Law in Other Jurisdictions

Courts in other jurisdictions have been reluctant to extend liability to gun manufacturers where the basis of liability is negligent manufacturing and distribution. California's Civil Code provides that no firearm shall be deemed defective under a product liability claim on the basis that the benefits of the firearm do not outweigh the societal risks and costs. The California Supreme Court has interpreted this statute strictly. *See Merrill v. Navegar, Inc.* (rejecting the plaintiff's attempt to bypass the statute, stating that the California Legislature's intent was to bar negligence claims involving risk/benefit analysis). Similarly, an Illinois Appellate Court rejected outright the idea of subjecting gun manufacturers to strict liability claims. *See Miller v. Civil Constructors, Inc.* (holding that because the risk of harm in using a firearm may be practically eliminated through the use of reasonable or utmost care, the imposition of strict liability would unnecessarily require the user to ensure complete safety regardless of the degree of care used).

The Texas Court of Appeals and the Florida Supreme Court, however, have recognized negligent entrustment as a basis for gun manufacturer liability. *See Kennedy v. Baird* (stating that a crucial element of a negligent entrustment claim is the degree of knowledge that the defendant had or should have had regarding the entrustee's ability to use the object in a dangerous and harmful manner); *Kitchen v. K-Mart Corp.* (holding that the defendant had the requisite knowledge required for negligent entrustment where the victim's boyfriend bought the gun at the defendant's store while intoxicated).

Market-share liability has been used in some jurisdictions. However, it has not been applied against gun manufacturers. The first notable application of market-share liability was in a California court. *See Sindell v. Abbott Laboratories.* The *Sindell* case involved DES, a generic drug produced by many manufacturers, which was found to cause cancer in the children of the mothers who ingested the drug. Given the time period that elapsed between the ingestion of the drug and the discovery of cancer, it was impossible to ascertain the identity of the specific manufacturer. The California Supreme Court's rationale for using market-share liability was that causation was impossible to establish given the unusual circumstances of the case and that the drug was a fungible product, which all of the defendants produced and manufactured in similar manners.

In contrast, Pennsylvania courts have never adopted market-share liability. *See Mellon v. Barre-National Drug Co.* In rejecting the plaintiff's claim of market-share liability against the manufacturers of an over-the-counter weight control drug, the District Court of Pennsylvania held that the facts of the case did not fit those of the DES cases. The court further held that the use of market-share liability should be a very narrow exception to the general rule that causation must be established, and because such unusual exceptions had not yet been brought in Pennsylvania court, the state did not accept the doctrine.

*"The right of the 'people' to keep and bear arms is a freedom that belongs not just to a select group of government-appointed bureaucrats, but to all Americans."*

# An Upset to Gun-Control Advocates

*Erich Pratt*

*Erich Pratt is the director of communications for Gun Owners of America. This national gun lobby, headquartered in Springfield, Virginia, includes 350,000 members. He has appeared on various radio and television programs, and has written a book titled* The Constitutional Recipe for Freedom: Twelve Principles of Liberty Today's Politicians Don't Want You to Know. *He received an MA in public policy from Regent University in 1988.*

*In this commentary published on the gun owners' Web site* Keep and Bear Arms, *Erich Pratt refers to gun-control advocates as "the inhabitants of Bradyville." The fictitious town alludes to the Brady Handgun Violence Prevention Act, a 1994 law that required background checks and a mandatory waiting period prior to the purchase of firearms. He discusses the setbacks that gun-control proponents have experienced in* Hamilton *and other cases. He argues that they want to bully gun manufacturers, that guns often save lives, and that the courts have upheld the right of Americans to own guns.*

Erich Pratt, "Gun Ruling Sends Shockwaves Through Bradyville," KeepAndBearArms .com, May 2, 2001. Copyright © 2001 Erich Pratt. Reproduced by permission of the author.

The inhabitants of Bradyville are up in arms these days.

Bradyville is the land of make-believe, where guns are thought to have magical powers. They are considered so evil that children have even been punished for waving a thumb and finger in the air—forming the shape of a gun—and saying "bang."

Yes, the inhabitants of Bradyville don't want guns in their town. And they have crafted all kinds of constitutional and legal theories to get them out of your town, too.

Well, New York's top court handed down a verdict on April 26 [2001] that has sent shockwaves rippling throughout the land [*Hamilton v. Beretta*]. The court ruled that gun makers can't be held liable when a bad guy uses one of their guns to kill someone.

That should be a no-brainer. After all, we don't hold General Motors liable when a wacko uses a Cadillac to intentionally run over children at a day-care center.

A situation like that actually happened in California two years ago [1999]. To date, no one in the media or in Congress has called upon the courts to stick it to the car industry. Yet, that is exactly what gun grabbers in Bradyville are trying to do to gun makers.

## Recent Setbacks for Gun-Control Advocates

The recent ruling out of New York, however, comes as a huge blow. Sarah Brady's foundation in the nation's capitol—which helped bring the lawsuit—declared the verdict a "setback."

Oh, but this was more than just a setback. The inhabitants of Bradyville have spent countless hours and untold dollars in courtrooms all across the nation to make this legal argument stick.

Nevertheless, they have suffered an almost complete string of losses. They are losing the suits that private individuals are bringing against gun manufacturers. They are losing the taxpayer-funded suits that 31 city and county governments have launched.

They have lost in states which are somewhat conservative—like Florida. And they have now lost in liberal courts like those in New York state.

So you have to wonder: if an extremely liberal New York court will not swallow the legal arguments coming from gun haters, then why should anyone else?

The judges from the Empire State warned that we should be cautious in imposing "novel" theories of law.

## Gun Opponents' Intentions

Still, the lawyers from Bradyville march on, spending thousands—perhaps millions—of dollars pursuing untried, novel theories. Why?

Quite simply, because they are not worried about losing in court.

What they really want is to financially cripple the dozens upon dozens of American businessmen who make a living selling a constitutionally protected item.

Edward Rendell lives in Bradyville. As the former mayor of Philadelphia and a previous head of the Democratic National Committee, he speaks for many of Bradyville's residents.

"The impact of so many cities filing suit all at once would be monumental for gun manufacturers," Rendell said. "They don't have the deep pockets of the tobacco industry, and it could bring them to the negotiating table a lot sooner."

You see, that's what they really want in Bradyville. They want to put a gun to the head of the gun makers, so to speak, and threaten them with extinction if they don't agree to negotiate . . . if they don't agree to preemptively swallow a vast gun control agenda.

Thus, their "novel" theory doesn't have to win in court. It only needs to bully the gun makers into submission.

So here's the $10 million question: if gun grabbers are willing to use "novel" legal theories to sink the American gun industry, what makes us think they aren't using "novel" theories when it comes to attacking the Second Amendment right to keep and bear arms?

What makes us think they don't skew the truth in order to sell us on gun bans, licensing and registration?

In Bradyville, they tell us the Constitution only protects firearms for those in the militia. They tell us guns are only for the National Guard. You and I don't have a constitutional right to keep arms for protection, they say.

But that's not what the Founding Fathers believed. Nor is it what a majority of the courts have stated over our more than 200-year history.

## Historical and Recent Positions

For example, James Madison—known as the Father of the Constitution—said in *Federalist Paper 46* that the Constitution preserves "the advantage of being armed, which the Americans possess over the people of almost every other nation . . . [where] the governments are afraid to trust the people with arms."

And more recently, the U.S. Supreme Court stated (in 1990) that the "people" mentioned in the Second Amendment are the same "people" mentioned elsewhere in the Bill of Rights.

This means that the right of the "people" to keep and bear arms is a freedom that belongs not just to a select group of government-appointed bureaucrats, but to all Americans.

Well, this need not strike fear into the hearts of Bradyville denizens. Guns are used more often to save lives than to take lives. And besides, guns really don't have magical powers. They are simply a tool, and on their own, can't walk down the street and shoot someone.

*"[The] claim of negligent marketing has been raised against handgun manufacturers ... where the product functions as intended, and as such is not defective in design, manufacture, or warnings."*

# Negligence Suits Against Gun Manufacturers Denied

*Frank J. Giliberti*

*Frank J. Giliberti is a partner in the Long Island office of the law firm Rivkin Radler LLP. He has experience representing corporations in product liability suits.*

*In the following selection, Frank J. Giliberti reviews the New York Court of Appeals decision in* Hamilton v. Beretta. *He details its impact on negligent marketing and distribution lawsuits against the gun industry, recognizing that "for the gun industry ... negligent marketing still remains primarily a theory." He also summarizes the key issues of the case and underlines the court's analysis of the manufacturers' duty to exercise reasonable care in the marketing of its products.*

Litigation over the marketing and advertising of products is not new. For years courts have recognized that companies can be held liable for false claims contained in their ads. Federal and state laws prohibiting "unfair methods of competition" and "unfair acts or practices" are often applied to marketers. Specific statutes governing particular forms of selling, such as telemarketing, can lead to court actions. And product liability lawsuits against manufacturers certainly aren't rare.

Recently, however, a relatively new kind of claim has arisen where plaintiffs contend a company's negligent marketing and distribution of its products led to injuries to the plaintiffs. This claim of negligent marketing has been raised against handgun manufacturers and other manufacturers where the product functions as intended, and as such is not defective in design, manufacture, or warnings. And virtually just as often, these claims have been rejected.

## Negligent Marketing

A few months ago [April 2001], New York State's top court, the court of Appeals, issued a decision in *Hamilton vs. Beretta U.S.A. Corp.* analyzing a negligent marketing claim brought against several gun manufacturers. Although the ruling arose in a case involving the gun industry, marketers of other products should take note because this opinion illustrates quite well how courts typically examine a negligent marketing claim and the hurdles facing plaintiffs who seek to recover damages under it.

## A Question of Duty

The case began when relatives of people killed by handguns alleged negligent marketing and sued various handgun manufacturers in a federal district court in New York. The plaintiffs asserted that the defendants had distributed their products negligently so as to create and bolster an illegal, underground handgun market that furnished weapons to minors and criminals.

These actions, they continued, violated the defendants' duty to exercise reasonable care in the marketing and distribution of their guns. The plaintiffs claimed that such a duty existed because of the defendants' ability to exercise control over the marketing and distribution of their guns, their general knowledge that large numbers of their guns entered the illegal market and were used in crime, New York's policy of strict regulation of firearms, and the uniquely lethal nature of these products.

## Claims of the Plaintiffs and Defendants

The plaintiffs also contended that the defendants controlled their distributors' conduct with respect to pricing, advertising, and display, yet refused to institute practices such as requiring distribution contracts that limited sales to gun dealers, training salespeople in safe sales practices (including how to recognize straw purchasers), establishing electronic monitoring of their products, limiting the number of distributors, limiting multiple purchases, and franchising their retail outlets.

The defendants countered they didn't have a duty to protect the public from the criminal acquisition and misuse of their handguns. The defendants asserted that such a duty potentially exposed them to limitless liability and shouldn't be imposed on them for acts and omissions of numerous and remote third parties whose actions they couldn't control. Further, they contended that, in light of the comprehensive statutory and regulatory scheme governing the distribution and sale of firearms, any fundamental changes in the industry should be left to the appropriate legislative and regulatory bodies.

After a four-week trial, the jury found that 15 of 25 defendants had failed to use reasonable care in the distribution of their guns. The district court upheld that determination, deciding that the defendants had a duty "to take reasonable steps available at the point of . . . sale to primary distributors to reduce the possibility that these instruments will fall into the hands of those likely to misuse them."

The court noted the defendants were able to detect and guard against any foreseeable risks associated with their products and said that ability created a special "protective relationship" between the manufacturers and potential victims of gun violence. The court noted that the relationship of handgun manufacturers with their downstream distributors and retailers gave them the authority and ability to control the latter's conduct for the protection of prospective crime victims. On appeal, the federal circuit court of appeals asked the New York Court of Appeals to explain whether the defendants could be held liable for negligent marketing under applicable New York law.

## What the Court Said

In its decision, the New York Court of Appeals indicated it was reluctant to impose a duty on gun manufacturers in this case because the pool of possible plaintiffs was so large—potentially including any of the thousands of victims of gun violence—and the connection between the defendants, the criminal wrongdoers, and the plaintiffs was so remote. "Such broad liability," the Court said, "potentially encompassing all gunshot crime victims, should not be imposed without a more tangible showing that the defendants were a direct link in the causal chain that resulted in the plaintiffs' injuries, and that the defendants were realistically in a position to prevent the wrongs."

The Court rejected the plaintiffs' argument that the gun manufacturers owed them a duty because of their "special ability" to detect and guard against the risks associated with their products. For one thing, the Court said, none of the plaintiffs' proof demonstrated that a change in the defendants' marketing techniques likely would have prevented their injuries. Indeed, the Court emphasized, the plaintiffs hadn't presented any evidence showing to what degree their risk of injury had been enhanced by the presence of negligently marketed and distributed guns, as opposed to the risk presented by all guns in society.

Neither was the Court impressed by the plaintiffs' assertions that a general duty of care arose out of the gun manufacturers' ability to reduce the risk of illegal gun trafficking through control of the marketing and distribution of their products. The district court had accepted this proposition and had posited a series of structural changes in defendants' marketing and distribution regimes that might reduce the risk of criminal misuse by ensuring that the first sale was by a responsible merchant to a responsible buyer.

## Federal District Court's Suggestions

For example, the district court suggested the defendants could limit the volume of sales in states with weak gun controls to ensure against circulation of the oversupply to strong gun control states such as New York; restrict distribution entirely to established retail stores carrying stocks of guns; franchise retail outlets; and bar distribution to dealers who sold at unregulated gun shows.

In the Court of Appeals' view, however, these changes would have the unavoidable effect of eliminating a significant number of lawful sales to "responsible" buyers by "responsible" federal firearms licensees who would be cut out of the distribution chain by the suggested actions. The Court stated, moreover, that the plaintiffs had presented no evidence showing any statistically significant relationship between particular classes of dealers and crime guns. "To impose a general duty of care upon the makers of firearms under these circumstances because of their purported ability to control marketing and distribution of their products would conflict with the principle that any judicial recognition of a duty of care must be based upon an assessment of its efficacy in promoting a social benefit as against its costs and burdens."

## Class of Plaintiffs and Defendants Would Be Too Numerous

In this case, the Court continued, imposing such a general duty of care would create not only an indeterminate class of plaintiffs, but also an indeterminate class of defendants "whose liability might have little relationship to the benefits of controlling illegal guns."

The Court also rejected the plaintiffs' final basis for imposing a duty of care: the so-called "negligent entrustment doctrine," arising out of the firearms manufacturers' authority over downstream distributors and retailers to whom their products were delivered. Under this doctrine, the owner or possessor of a dangerous instrument is under a duty to entrust it to a responsible person whose use doesn't create an unreasonable risk of harm to others. The duty may extend through successive, reasonably anticipated entrustees.

The Court pointed out a number of fatal impediments to imposing a general duty of care in this case under a negligent entrustment theory. The Court said this theory was inappropriate in this case because the plaintiffs hadn't presented evidence indicating that the manufacturer knew or had reason to know their distributors were engaging in substantial sales of guns into the gun-trafficking market on a consistent basis. Instead the plaintiffs had claimed that manufacturers shouldn't engage in certain broad categories of sales. But without a showing that specific groups of dealers played a disproportionate role in supplying the illegal gun market, "the sweep of plaintiffs' duty theory is far wider than the danger it seeks to avert," the Court held. The Court then concluded that the defendants didn't owe the plaintiffs the duty they claimed.

## Impact of New York Court of Appeals Decision

If the plaintiffs had been able to provide the evidence the New York Court of Appeals mentioned, the Court may have reached a different result. Moreover, there may be situations where a manufacturer has actual control over a third party or has a relationship with a plaintiff that requires the manufacturer to protect the plaintiff from the conduct of others. The defendant's relationship with either the third party or the plaintiff places the defendant in the best position to protect against the risk of harm. However, this duty doesn't extend beyond that limited class of plaintiffs to members of the community at large.

In cases involving the distribution or handling of hazardous materials, the courts have imposed a heightened duty of care on manufacturers. In these cases, the manufacturer's duty is, however, still based either on the theory that the product was defective because of a failure to include a safety feature or provide appropriate warnings about the dangers of the product to downstream distributors and sellers who may have more direct contact with the end user.

Certainly, too, a manufacturer may be held liable for complicity in dangerous or illegal activity. Courts, however, haven't been persuaded that these arguments should apply to the handgun industry based merely upon the usual and customary legal marketing and sales practices. They also typically reject product liability claims against gun manufacturers because their products generally are not defective—if anything, the problem is they work too well.

## Negligent Marketing Only Theory

For now at least, the courts have dismissed negligent marketing claims against handgun manufacturers. This isn't to say that plaintiffs won't be able to develop evidence to demonstrate a particular gun manufacturer could have taken reasonable steps to prevent their injuries through more responsible marketing practices. However, for the gun industry and other manufacturers where no specific evidence exists indicating an unwarranted or negligent departure from legal sale and distribution, negligent marketing still remains primarily a theory. Whether it will be a viable tool for future plaintiffs will be determined on a case-by-case basis.

> *"The ability to sue is necessary to hold gun manufacturers and dealers responsible for negligent practices that result in shooting deaths."*

# The Federal Law Shielding Gun Manufacturers from Lawsuits

## David Dean

*At the time he originally published this article in 2005, David Dean was a student at the New York University School of Law. He previously worked as a policy analyst for the New York City Mayor's Office of the Criminal Justice Coordinator.*

*In the following essay, David Dean expresses concern that the Protection of Lawful Commerce in Arms Act, a 2005 law that prevents gun manufacturers and dealers from being held accountable for crimes committed with their products, has too broadly exempted the gun industry from liability, before the nation had a chance to see whether the lawsuits now prohibited by the law could have had an effect on gun crime and negligent or unsafe sales practices. He wonders whether the act will specifically damage the efforts by New York City to cut down on guns in the city, with its local law—passed before the federal act— that permitted gun-violence victims to sue arms manufacturers and retailers that did not have strict standards "to prevent illegal trafficking" in place. Furthermore, Dean points out, the law may not have even been necessary, given that the courts were already*

David Dean, "Gun Control and the New Federal Law Shielding Gun Manufacturers from Lawsuits," *Gotham Gazette: New York City News and Policy*, November 1, 2005. Reproduced by permission.

*routinely rejecting lawsuits against manufacturers that were without substantial merit.*

When President George W. Bush signed the newly-passed Protection of Lawful Commerce in Arms Act into law on October 26th [2005], it marked a major victory for the National Rifle Association and gun manufacturers, who have been pushing for the legislation for years. It also marked a tremendous defeat for New York City and the many other cities that have pending lawsuits against the gun industry.

The law is specifically designed to end those lawsuits. It specifically exempts firearm manufacturers, distributors, dealers, and importers from civil liability for injuries and deaths caused by their products (it was quite a week for shielding big business, as the House of Representatives also passed the so-called "Cheeseburger Bill," which prohibits lawsuits against fast food restaurants for causing obesity). While the law allows lawsuits in the case of a defective gun or criminal conduct by a manufacturer or dealer, it prohibits lawsuits of the kind filed by numerous individuals and municipalities, including New York City, and calls for any pending suits to be dismissed immediately.

The Protection of Lawful Commerce in Arms Act is also likely to frustrate local efforts to control the flow of guns into New York City. The City Council passed a law in January [2005] that allows victims of gun violence to sue gun manufacturers and dealers who have not adopted strict standards to prevent illegal trafficking. Manufacturers and dealers that abide by those standards are exempt from being sued. While the city's lawyers will likely argue otherwise, it is likely that the new federal law effectively overturns the city's law.

Supporters of shielding the gun industry from liability argue that it is necessary to protect firearms manufacturers from "frivolous" and "reckless" lawsuits designed to bankrupt the gun industry. Opponents, on the other hand, argue that the ability to sue is necessary to hold gun manufacturers and dealers responsible for negligent practices that result in shooting deaths.

## Brief Issue in the Mayoral Campaign

Fallout from the law's passage even entered into the [2005] mayoral campaign. Fernando Ferrer criticized Mayor Michael Bloomberg's contributions to six members of Congress who voted to pass the bill, and suggested that the mayor had "joined the gun lobby." In criticizing the law and the mayor, Ferrer pointed out that shootings have increased by six percent this year over the same period in 2004, even as crime in the city has decreased overall. Bloomberg, who had lobbied against the new law, released a statement after the bill passed, calling it "a disgraceful piece of legislation" that "will make it easier for criminals to get firearms and put our law enforcement officers at greater risk."

## Are the Lawsuits Effective in Preventing Gun Violence?

At best, it remains an open question whether the recent spate of lawsuits is an effective way to deter gun crime. Opponents of gun control argue that there is no evidence to suggest that gun control reduces violent crime, and that it may in fact increase crime by taking guns out of the hands of law-abiding citizens. Lawsuits, they say, are an attempt by gun control advocates to bankrupt gun manufacturers.

However, the lawsuits that have been filed against the gun industry in recent years have been focused not on gun sales to law abiding citizens, but against what the suits claim is negligent behavior by gun manufacturers and dealers that allows guns to wind up in the hands of criminals. Evidence suggests that a small number of dealers are responsible for selling a majority of the guns used in crimes.

New York City's lawsuit attempted to show that many of the guns used in crimes here in New York are originally sold in states with weaker gun control laws and brought to the city illegally. For example, the *New York Post* reported on October 15th [2005] that authorities had arrested a man suspected of bringing as many as 75 illegal firearms into New York City in less than a year. The suspect was allegedly part of a ring that purchased the guns in Virginia and sold them on the streets of New York. Virginia recently weakened a state law limiting the number of handguns a single individual could purchase in a month, a law initially passed in an attempt to curb gun smuggling.

The theory behind the litigation is similar to efforts in recent decades to use lawsuits to improve the safety of a number of consumer goods, from automobiles to children's toys. Individuals and cities filing these lawsuits hope to give gun manufacturers and dealers the financial incentive to do what they can to prevent this illegal gun trafficking.

## Is the Liability Shield Necessary?

While proponents of shielding gun manufacturers from lawsuits argue that such a measure is needed to discourage frivolous lawsuits, the irony is that the legal system has been doing a good job, in New York City and elsewhere, of weeding out the lawsuits that are without merit. In 2001, for instance, New York's highest court, the Court of Appeals, overturned a Brooklyn jury's verdict that had awarded close to four million dollars in damages to Stephen Fox, who was permanently disabled after being shot by a friend. In the case, *Hamilton v. Beretta U.S.A.* [2001], the court argued in part that "the connection between defendants, the criminal wrongdoers and plaintiffs is remote, running through several links in a chain," and thus legal liability for the manufacturers was inappropriate. Similarly, a federal judge in Brooklyn dismissed a suit brought by the National Association for the Advancement of Colored People (NAACP), saying that the organization had failed to prove its public nuisance claim against the gun industry's marketing practices. And a New York State appellate court found the trial court had properly dismissed another nuisance lawsuit, this one filed by Attorney General Eliot Spitzer on behalf of the state.

Yet the lawsuit filed by New York City seemed to have avoided the problems that doomed the attempts by Stephen Fox, the NAACP, and New York State. In fact, the same judge that dismissed the NAACP's suit allowed the city's to go forward. Now that the Protection of Lawful Commerce in Arms Act has become law, it is likely only a matter of time before the city's suit is also dismissed. Any attempt to invoke the local law passed by the City Council in January is also likely to fail.

Gun control opponents could be right when they claim that lawsuits against the gun industry will not reduce gun crimes. Now, because of the new liability shield law, New York City will not have an opportunity to find out.

> "Responsibility and control of the actions of gun retailers lie squarely with the federal government and the retailers themselves, not with manufacturers."

# Congress Was Justified in Passing the Protection of Lawful Commerce in Arms Act

*Charley Reese*

*Charley Reese entered the journalism field in the 1950s, during which decade he also served as a tank gunner in the U.S. Army for two years. He worked on various political campaigns in several states between 1969 and 1971 and was an editor and writer for the* Orlando Sentinel *from 1971 to 2001. He has continued to write as a syndicated columnist.*

*In this essay, Charley Reese applauds the Protection of Lawful Commerce in Arms Act and voices his distrust of the gun-control lobby, arguing that its intention is to abolish private gun ownership and bankrupt gun manufacturers. Reese writes that manufacturers have no control over or knowledge of what people will do with their products and thus cannot be held liable. He holds that the right to arms and the freedom of U.S. citizens go hand in hand and that if the former is taken away, so is the latter.*

Charley Reese, "Keep the Canary Alive," *LewRockwell.com*, November 1, 2005. Copyright © 2005 by King Features Syndicate, Inc. Reprinted with Special Permission of North America Syndicate.

Congress finally did something right, and we should all applaud. The Senate and the House passed a law that shields gun manufacturers from politically-motivated lawsuits [Protection of Lawful Commerce in Arms Act, 2005].

I just read a rant by a liberal columnist on the subject, and as usual, in his hysteria, he got the facts wrong. The new law, which President Bush is expected to sign, does not exempt gun manufacturers from lawsuits. If they produce a defective product that causes injury, they can still be sued. All the new law does is put them on a level playing field with every other manufacturer.

## The Anti-Gun Lobby's Intentions

You hear a lot about the gun lobby, mainly the National Rifle Association, of which I am proud to be a life member. There is also, however, an anti-gun lobby that over time has masqueraded under different names. Its goal is to abolish the private ownership of firearms. The lobby doesn't openly admit it, but that's its aim.

With rare exceptions in a few cities and states in which no decent American should live, the anti-gun lobby has failed miserably through the democratic process. If the lobby was honest, which it is not, it would simply seek the repeal of the Second Amendment. Instead, it tries roundabout ways to accomplish the goal of disarming the populace.

Lawsuits against gun manufacturers were intended to bankrupt the companies. These lawsuits were so ridiculous that if we had a decent class of judges, they would have been thrown out without even a hearing. A mayor in New Orleans some years ago sued gun manufacturers in an attempt to blame them for the city's sorry crime rate. Other suits try to blame the manufacturers for the actions of criminals in individual cases.

## Civil Litigation Involving
## Other Manufacturers

Before America's exceedingly excessive number of lawyers corrupted the civil-court system, the principles involved in liability were simple and logical. You can't be held liable for something over which you have no control. A manufacturer has no control over or even knowledge of the behavior of the end user of his product. The fact that these lawsuits were politically motivated is shown by the absence of such suits against other manufacturers.

Nobody has sued Ford Motor Co. because some Ford owner uses his car to rob banks or kidnap children or run down pedestrians. Nor should you be able to sue Smith & Wesson because some crackhead uses one of its pistols to commit murder. As I said, all of these lawsuits should have been immediately dismissed, but because of the low quality of so many judges, many of them were not. Even when the manufacturers win, as they have so far, the legal costs are exorbitant. And that was the strategy of the anti-gun lobby—to bleed the companies with endless lawsuits.

## The Responsibilities of Manufacturers,
## Retailers, Individuals, and the Government

America's gun manufacturers produce some of the highest-quality products in the world. They are safe. Manufacturers sell to wholesalers, who sell to retailers, who in turn sell to individual customers. Some of these suits tried to blame manufacturers for the actions of retailers. That was stupid on its face.

All gun retailers in the United States are licensed and regulated by the federal government. Agents of the Bureau of Alcohol, Tobacco and Firearms have the authority to walk into any retailer at any time without notice and thoroughly inspect all of the records and inventory. If any retailer is engaged in hanky-panky, and the overwhelming majority are not, that is the fault and responsibility of the federal government, not the manufacturer.

To buy the anti-gun ploy would be like holding General Motors responsible for the behavior of every used-car salesman who sold a secondhand GM car. Responsibility and control of the actions of gun retailers lie squarely with the federal government and the retailers themselves, not with manufacturers.

Machiavelli once remarked that the Swiss were the "most armed and most free" people in Europe. When the day comes that your government tells you it is forbidden for you to own and keep a firearm, you will no longer be living in a free country. A government that is afraid of its own citizens is undemocratic and authoritarian. The Second Amendment is the canary that monitors our freedom. When it dies, freedom dies. Even if you don't wish to own a firearm, you should join the National Rifle Association and defend the Second Amendment against those who want the government to have a monopoly on force.

*"That no other industry gets this special legal protection regarding the liability derived from the harm caused by their products is ... alarming."*

# An Overview of the Suits Against Gun Manufacturers

## Mireia Artigot i Golobardes

*Mireia Artigot i Golobardes is an assistant professor at Pompeu Fabra University in Barcelona, Spain. She received her LLM from Cornell Law School in 2002 and is completing her JSD from the same school. She has bachelor's degrees in law and economics and business administration, and included among her other articles is "Product Liability and Product Safety in Europe: A Coordination of Incentive Schemes Is Needed."*

*Here Mireia Artigot i Golobardes discusses the Protection of Lawful Commerce in Arms Act as well as the events that precipitated its passage and the implications it has for future litigation with regard to gun control, gun safety, and manufacturers' and retailers' responsibilities. She posits that the law is a positive step in preventing frivolous lawsuits but also finds that the manner and degree to which the government is protecting the gun industry with this law, in ways it does not protect other industries whose products may cause harm, is disconcerting.*

During the last ten years, there has been an exponential raise in suits brought against gun manufacturers and distributors.

Mireia Artigot i Golobardes, "Slowly but Surely: The U.S. Congress' Attempt to Shield Gun Manufacturers from Liability," *Indret.com*, January, 2006. Reproduced by permission.

154

Until now, most of these claims have been dismissed in favor of defendants by courts that have understood that these claims did not state a cause of action either under product liability theories, negligence and negligent entrustment, public nuisance or market share liability.

In October 1998, however, the tendency changed and private citizens were joined by municipalities such as New Orleans, that became the first municipality to file a suit against the gun industry. Since then many cities in the U.S. have sued manufacturers, distributors or other participants of the gun industry. One of the latest cases has taken place in New York, where in 2004 New York city sued the gun manufacturers and sellers for creating a public nuisance by marketing and distributing firearms in ways that make them accessible to criminals.

These suits represented a first step adopted by victims together with municipalities in trying to claim damages against gun manufacturers for the harm caused by firearms. However, even though some Congressmen had manifested their position towards these lawsuits, up to now the legislative power had not made explicit its standpoint regarding the scope of liability to which gun manufacturers should be exposed to.

The difficulty to success in these lawsuits and in receiving compensation for the harm suffered implied that victims and their attorneys used legal theories that were not meant to be applied in this context. For this reason, despite the victims' energy and imagination, they were generally unsuccessful in their claims. There was still hope, though.

## Passage of the Protection of Lawful Commerce in Arms Act

However, on October 26, 2005, Congress passed the Protection of Lawful Commerce in Arms Act, which seeks to protect firearms manufacturers from being sued for the criminal misuse of their lawful products by third parties. This legislation seeks to prevent abuses to the American legal system from frivolous lawsuits.

This brief note will present an overview of the origin and the evolution of the suits filed against gun manufacturers and continue with a concise presentation of the content of this ... act. In an earlier paper ... I claimed that ... despite the lack of specific regulation applicable to these lawsuits against gun manufacturers, the existing legal theories should not be streched in such cases because this was not the role of courts and judges but of the legislature.

However, the situation now is quite different given that it seems that Congress has decided to protect the firearms industry from these lawsuits based on the understanding that a significant amount of them are frivolous, by making it very difficult for victims to bring a claim against gun manufacturers for the harm suffered by guns.

Even though this Act has just been passed and it is difficult to assess its impact and its interaction with state regulation in light of its current lack of application, it is still worth presenting this new regulation recently passed by the U.S. Congress.

I will now briefly present an overview of the different legal theories upon which lawsuits against gun manufacturers were brought. I believe that this will allow us to better assess and understand the potential impact of the Protection of Lawful Commerce in Arms Act. . . .

## Products Liability Grounds

The first suits against gun manufacturers were brought as products liability claims. However, product liability does not impose liability for dangerous products as such but only for the harm caused by products that are deemed to be defective—either because of a manufacturing defect, a defect on the product design or a defect based on the failure to warn or to instruct. Guns are not defective products, just dangerous, and this resulted in product claims against gun manufacturers being dismissed unless the gun was proved to be defective.

## Negligence Grounds

In light of the failure of product liability theories, plaintiffs sought alternative theories in order to hold gun manufacturers liable, including the traditional negligence concept of tort law. Concretely, plaintiffs focused on the conduct of defendants and alleged gun manufacturers' negligent marketing.

In order to sustain a negligence claim, plaintiffs must show the *prima facie* elements of negligent conduct. These elements are the existence of a legal duty of care, a breach of the duty, the existence of damages resulting from this breach and that the manufacturer's breach of the duty was the proximate cause of the plaintiff's harm. However, legal policy requires that "courts must be mindful of the precedential, and consequential, future effects of their rulings, and 'limit the legal consequences of wrongs to a controllable degree [*Lauer v. City of New York*].'" In other words, courts must determine the scope of this duty as well.

Generally, plaintiffs' suits against gun manufacturers under the negligent marketing theory did not prevail because of major causation and duty problems.

Imposing a general duty of care upon the makers of firearms under these circumstances based on their supposed ability to control the marketing and the distribution process of their products would conflict with the principle that any judicial recognition of a duty of care must be based upon an assessment of its efficacy in promoting a social benefit as against its costs and burdens.

The major problem in imposing a duty on gun manufacturers is that it is very difficult, if not impossible, to define its scope given that a duty may not be predicated just because it is foreseeable that persons may be killed or injured by defendants' lethal products. Victims of illegal handguns could not show that a change in the marketing techniques would likely have prevented their injuries.

Therefore, imposing such duty could create an indeterminate class of plaintiffs as well as an indeterminate class of defendants whose liability might have little relationship to the benefits of controlling illegal guns.

Consequently, given the difficulty to define the scope of this duty and how difficult it is for courts to distinguish between cases where a gun has been properly distributed from cases where a gun has been distributed improperly and ended in the hands of future criminals, courts generally considered that gun manufacturers owed no duty to insure against third parties for the criminal use of their non-defective products.

## Grounds of Negligent Entrustment

An alternative basis for imposing a duty of care was the negligent entrustment doctrine, based on the supposed authority of firearms manufacturers over "downstream distributors and retailers" to whom they deliver their products.

The tort of negligent entrustment is based on the degree of knowledge the supplier of a chattel has or should have regarding the entrustee's propensity to use the chattel in an improper or dangerous manner. In this sense, the owner or possessor of a dangerous instrument is under a duty to entrust it to a responsible person whose use does not create an unreasonable risk of harm to others. This tort interacts with Federal law that has already implemented a statutory and regulatory scheme to ensure the seller's "responsibility" through licensing requirements and buyer's "responsibility" through required background checks.

Courts have considered that the negligent entrustment doctrine might well support the extension of a duty to manufacturers through successive, reasonably anticipated entrustees. This extension seeks to avoid selling to certain distributors in circumstances where the manufacturer knows or has reason to know those distributors are engaging in substantial sales of guns into the gun-trafficking market on a consistent basis.

Thus, gun suppliers have been subjected to liability under this theory as long as they knew or should have known the individual's ability to use the gun safely.

However, general statements or claiming that manufacturers about an industry are not enough to establish that the gun supplier's duty. Therefore, stating that gun manufacturers should not engage in certain categories of sales is not enough given that defendants do not have an affirmative duty to investigate and identify corrupt dealers, which would not be feasible anyway. Courts have required showing that specific groups of dealers play a disproportionate role in supplying the illegal gun market, otherwise the defendant's duty would become far wider than the danger it seeks to prevent.

## The Market Share Liability Theory

Plaintiffs have also tried to use the market share liability theory, which proves an exception to the general rule that in common-law negligence. Under this theory, a plaintiff must prove that the defendant's conduct was a cause-in-fact of the injury. However, in order to apply the market share liability theory, Courts have required that products are fungible and that it is not possible to identify the manufacturer of the product that caused the injury to a particular plaintiff.

Courts have considered that this liability theory is not adequate in this firearms context given that it is often possible to identify the type of firearms and its manufacturer and the marketing techniques of the different gun manufacturers are not uniform—gun manufacturers have different marketing activities that allegedly contribute to the illegal handgun market in different ways and to different extents. Therefore, simple apportionment would not lead to a fair result. Courts in New York and other jurisdictions have refused to extend the market share theory where products were not fungible and differing degrees of risk were created because the manufacturer's share of the national handgun market does not necessarily correspond to the amount of risk created by its alleged tortious conduct.

Furthermore, there is a significant difficulty in proving precisely which manufacturer caused any particular plaintiff's injuries since guns used in crimes are often not recovered. The inability to locate evidence, however, does not alone justify the extraordinary step of applying market share liability. Rather, a more compelling policy reason is required for the imposition of market share liability.

## Nuisance Grounds

In light of the failure of the traditional tort categories to hold gun manufacturers liable, plaintiffs' lawyers thought that nuisance was a broadly defined tort whose flexible crime-fighting content could allow them to state causes of action against gun manufacturers.

In the Restatement (Second) of Torts, nuisance is used to refer to the harm to another or to the invasion of an interest and specifically states that "nuisance" does not signify any particular kind of conduct on the part of the defendant. Instead, the concept of nuisance refers to two particular kinds of harm—the invasion of two kinds of interests—by conduct that is tortious only if it falls into the usual categories of tort liability.

Public nuisance focuses on the rights of the general public rather than the rights of particular people harmed. This doctrine has been used in the environmental, the asbestos and the tobacco litigation context. However, the new litigation focus is the gun cases. Recent judicial decisions have rejected nuisance as a basis for liability in these cases because courts have considered that if defective products are not a nuisance as a matter of law, it would not make any sense to consider a nondefective, lawful product as a nuisance.

Municipalities believed that manufacturers of guns facilitated, sustained and sometimes even encouraged the demand for their products for their use in criminal acts. By doing that, municipalities believed that gun manufacturers promoted guns to everybody else as necessary for their protection against guns used by criminals and that this conduct constituted public nuisance. The basis of those claims was the direct, foreseeable and known harm done to the cities by marketing, distributing and promoting policies and practices of gun manufacturers and therefore making them available for the purposes of committing a crime. In the few cases brought by individuals against gun manufacturers based on public nuisance, the defendants' motions to dismiss were granted.

Regardless of whether these public nuisance claims are brought defending the population against risks posed by firearms or as a direct plaintiff who suffers losses, whether the actions of the gun industry constitute public nuisance is crucial to the outcome of these suits because if successful, the government tools for crime control would be significantly increased.

## New York City Suit on Public Nuisance Grounds

However, this situation may start changing in New York and from there, in other cities throughout the U.S.

In 2004 New York City sued the gun manufacturers and sellers for creating public nuisance by marketing and distributing firearms in ways that make the accessibility of handguns prevalent to criminals. Judge Jack B. Weinstein of the U.S. District Court for the Eastern District of New York found that New York law permits the City to bring lawsuits against gun manufacturers and sellers for creating public nuisance. The City's current complaint seeks no damages but instead requests an injunction requiring the defendants to adopt responsible business practices. However, this lawsuit is still pending at this time [January 2006].

Admitting that this claim already states a cause of action of public nuisance is already very important but the outcome of this lawsuit is of crucial importance for the future evolution of the lawsuits against gun manufacturers and more generally the firearms industry as a whole, because it may open the possibility to prevail against gun manufacturers for the harm caused by their non-defective products.

It is too early, though, to foresee how this lawsuit will turn up. However, anticipating this possibility, Congress has stepped in and significantly protected and helped the firearm industry by recently enacting the Protection of Lawful Commerce in Arms Act.

## The Legislature's and Court's Responsibilities

Based on the separation of powers established in the U.S. Constitution, judges and courts are not designed and qualified for determining whether certain activities that are completely legal impose too much risk to citizens through the application of legal theories not meant for this purpose.

I believe that it is the legislative power the one with the authority to establish the mechanisms to determine that a product is inherently dangerous and therefore should be kept out of the market or whether should be legally marketed but by participants of the industry internalizing the costs of the harm caused. It is the responsibility of the legislature to determine the policy regarding commerce and therefore to set gun laws, and the job of the judiciary to interpret that policy and ensure that the constitutional integrity is maintained.

When an older article involving this issue was published in [In Dret], U.S. Congress had not made an explicit statement regarding the liability of the firearms industry and the tendency of the lawsuits filed against some gun manufacturers. However, the context and the general framework of this situation is completely different for two major reasons.

First, courts have started to allow bringing legal claims against gun manufacturers that attempted to hold them liable. In this sense, Courts have begun to be sensitive to seller's responsibility regarding harm caused by guns sold for example, illegally or to criminals and have started to take steps to prevent such bad commerce and bad use of guns.

At the same time and despite the National Rifle Association efforts to silence this issue, courts have started to point out the legal gap regarding gun safety given that guns are one of the few products—if not the only one—not subject to any specific safety regulation.

In light of this situation, it can be considered a great success for the industry the Protection of Lawful Commerce in Arms Act. . . given that from a practical perspective, it is possible to fear that it closes the door of U.S. courthouses to firearms victims.

## Does the Act Provide Immunity to the Gun Industry?

Some say, and there are grounds supporting such conclusion, that this bill provides immunity to the firearm industry in the U.S. However such conclusion might be too premature.

A similar measure had previously been rejected by the U.S. Senate on March 2, 2004 but on October 26, 2005 this bill was passed. This Act aims to address the increasing number of pending lawsuits brought both by individuals and by municipalities against gun manufacturers whose products are used to commit a violent crime.

This bill, though, is very protective of the firearms industry given that it prevents victims of gun-related crimes from suing gun makers and dealers and therefore makes significantly harder holding gun manufacturers liable when their products are used to commit a crime given that it prohibits bringing any liability claim against gun makers and dealers in any state or federal court while requires dismissing any pending actions against them.

Citing the specific words of the bill, firearm victims cannot file a lawsuit against manufacturers or sellers of firearms, ammunition, or components of a firearm for the damages they suffered as a consequence of the "criminal or unlawful misuse of a firearm." So for example, a gun manufacturer would not be liable if a criminal uses one of the weapons he manufactures and kills a number of people or, for example, if a gun dealer does not keep track of his inventory and some guns disappear and without reporting this to the authorities; these guns are used to commit crimes resulting in deaths.

## Exceptions by Which Manufacturers and Retailers May Be Held Liable

This bill, though, includes some exceptions that would hold gun manufacturers liable: in cases where the person or persons who sell or transfer the firearm do so knowingly that it will be used in the commission of a crime of violence or in a drug trafficking crime; where federal or state laws are violated in the transfer of the firearms and the violation is the proximate cause of the harm for which relief is sought; where there is a breach of contract or warranty in connection with the purchase of the firearm and in cases of death, physical injuries, or property damage resulting directly from a defect in design or manufacture of the firearm when this is used as intended or in a reasonably foreseeable manner.

Given how popular firearms fairs are in little U.S. towns, the interpretation and application of this provision that opens a slight opportunity to hold gun manufacturers liable, will be crucial for these lawsuits.

However, the fact that no other industry gets this special legal protection regarding the liability derived from the harm caused by their products is already too alarming for not commenting this Act.

It is far too early to foresee how the interpretation and implementation of this provision and of the whole act will be and whether it will be considered constitutional or not. Even though the opinions where this exception has been challenged have not been released at this time while I am writing this note, it has been key already in certain lawsuits and this seems to be just the beginning.

Even though this act raises many issues regarding the Congress' standpoint concerning the degree and the circumstances under which gun manufacturers should be held liable, it will not be until later in time when we will be able to assess the impact of this act that has just been passed.

## The Benefits of the Act and the Concerns Raised by It

As mentioned in a previous article, the legislature—and not the courts—should be deciding which activities will be considered legal and socially necessary activities and therefore whether the costs derived from them will be borne by the society as a whole; and which costs derived from them should be borne by the different agents participating in that industry, instead of holding liable the participants of a certain legal and heavily regulated industry of the costs derived from their legally marketed product. Therefore, I believe that the explicit step adopted by Congress is very valuable in order to prevent filing frivolous lawsuits against gun manufacturers. Even if I disagree with the current wording and the content of the Protection of Lawful Commerce in Arms Act, I believe that it is not good judicial policy streching and using existing tort categories inadequately in order to be able to hold gun manufacturers liable, even in cases where the defendant's conduct does not fit in any tortious conduct subject to liability. Doing so would represent an inadequate and discretional application of the existing legal instruments.

However, in light of the remarkable amount of victims of firearms in the U.S. and the important problem of violence existing in the U.S., it is kind of disappointing to witness the

Act passed by Congress and therefore the position adopted, which is possible to interpret as an important victory of U.S. conservative groups and of the gun industry as a whole.

# CHAPTER 4

# Maintaining the Right to Keep and Bear Arms

# Chapter Preface

## Case Overview: *United States v. Emerson* (2001)

In *United States v. Emerson*, the Court had before it the questions of whether the Second Amendment applies to individuals and, if so, to what extent such rights can be restricted, defined, and narrowed. At issue were the Second Amendment and the statute 18 U.S.C. §922(g)(8), often referred to as the Violence Against Women Act, which prohibits anyone under a restraining order because of harassment or threatening language or behavior from possessing a firearm.

In August 1998 Sacha Emerson filed for divorce from Timothy Joe Emerson and requested a court order, restraining Timothy Emerson from harming or threatening her or their young daughter. At a subsequent hearing, Sacha Emerson provided evidence that Timothy had previously threatened Sacha with killing one of her friends. Timothy Emerson had notice of the hearing but did not offer any rebuttal evidence, and after ten days, on September 14, 1998, the judge issued the court order prohibiting Timothy from threatening or physically harming Sacha Emerson or her daughter.

In the following weeks, Timothy Emerson continued to make threats and in November physically threatened Sacha and their daughter with a 9mm pistol. He told police officers that he had an AK-47 assault rifle. Emerson was thus indicted in the Northern District of Texas on December 8, 1998, on five counts. The government chose to move forward on only one count, of unlawfully possessing a firearm in violation of the Violence Against Women Act. Emerson moved to dismiss, arguing that the statute in question violated the Second Amendment and the Due Process Clause of the Fifth Amendment. He further argued that this case was an improper use of federal power under the Commerce Clause and that the Tenth Amendment gave the power in these matters to the states. The district court subsequently dismissed the case on the basis of Emerson's cited Second and Fifth Amendment grounds. The government appealed to the Fifth Circuit Court of Appeals.

The Fifth Circuit's opinion, written by Judge William Garwood, focused substantially on the matter of Second Amendment models and individual rights versus collective rights before coming to its conclusion in favor of the government, reversing the district court's dismissal of the case. Garwood examined in great detail the various interpretations of the Second Amendment, discussing at length the definitions, meanings, and contexts of various Second Amendment terms.

He ultimately concluded that the Second Amendment does protect individual rights—but not universally. In the case of *Emerson*, the court ruled, the right could be restricted. Individual rights may be protected, Garwood wrote, but "that does not mean that those rights may never be made subject to any limited, narrowly tailored specific exceptions or restrictions for particular cases that are reasonable and not inconsistent with the right of Americans generally." The court also rejected Emerson's Due Process claim because he had received notice regarding the restraining order, had appeared at the hearing, and had never made any efforts to argue against it.

The opinion proved controversial for various reasons, not the least of which was, indeed, the substantial energy and number of pages devoted to, arguably unnecessarily, interpreting the Second Amendment's meaning. The majority opinion itself was accompanied by a "specially concurring" opinion by Judge Robert M. Parker, who took exception to Garwood's use of the opinion to so lengthily examine the individual rights-versus-collective rights debate and even make a conclusion. Parker pointed out that this part of the opinion—in which Garwood wrote rather openly that the Second Amendment does guarantee an individual right to gun ownership—was not necessary to the opinion in this case and was therefore *dicta*, or an opinion not relevant or necessary to the case at hand and therefore not binding case law either. He criticized Garwood for overstepping his bounds, when judges' "special charge" is "to avoid constitutional questions when the outcome of the case does not turn on how we answer." *Emerson* represented the first time a court had so clearly defined the Second Amendment as providing an individual right to keep and bear arms, but because the analysis is non-binding and arguably irrelevant dicta, it presents a problem: although many see it as a judge's opinion that was unnecessarily inserted into an opinion and that holds no binding weight, others may invoke it, whether officially or unofficially, as precedent to be followed.

> "Although the Second Amendment does
> protect individual rights, that does not
> mean that those rights may never be
> made subject to ... exceptions or re-
> strictions."

# The Court's Decision: The Second Amendment Applies to Individuals

## Judge William Garwood

*Judge William Garwood, a graduate of Princeton University and the University of Texas School of Law, started his career clerking for Judge John R. Brown of the U.S. Fifth Circuit Court of Appeals. In subsequent years he served as a JAG officer, worked in private practice, and held an appointment to the Texas Supreme Court before being nominated in 1981 by President Ronald Reagan to the Fifth Circuit Court of Appeals, where he had started his career some twenty-five years before.*

*In the Fifth Circuit's opinion in* United States v. Emerson, *Judge William Garwood spends much of the opinion disagreeing with and ruling against the government's arguments before ultimately reversing the lower court's ruling anyway, for different reasons. After discussing the various models of Second Amendment interpretation and examining the facts of the* Emerson *case, the court found that the Second Amendment does protect individual rights but that in particular cases—such as* Emerson—*it is not in violation of the Second Amendment for the legal system to limit or restrict the right of a specific individual.*

Judge William Garwood, majority opinion, *United States v. Emerson*, U.S. Fifth Circuit Court of Appeals, October 16, 2001.

The Second Amendment provides:

"A well regulated Militia, being necessary to the security of a free State, the right of the people to keep and bear arms, shall not be infringed."

The district court held that the Second Amendment recognizes the right of individual citizens to own and possess firearms, and declared that section 922(g)(8) was unconstitutional on its face because it requires that a citizen be disarmed merely because of being subject to a "boilerplate [domestic relations injunction] order with no particularized findings." The government opines that *stare decisis* [Latin legal term meaning precedent decisions are to be followed by the courts] requires us to reverse the district court's embrace of the individual rights model. Amici for the government argue that even if binding precedent does not require reversal, the flaws in the district court's Second Amendment analysis do.

## An Overview of Second Amendment Models

In the last few decades, courts and commentators have offered what may fairly be characterized as three different basic interpretations of the Second Amendment. The first is that the Second Amendment does not apply to individuals; rather, it merely recognizes the right of a state to arm its militia. This "states' rights" or "collective rights" interpretation of the Second Amendment has been embraced by several of our sister circuits. The government commended the states' rights view of the Second Amendment to the district court, urging that the Second Amendment does not apply to individual citizens.

Proponents of the next model admit that the Second Amendment recognizes some limited species of individual right. However, this supposedly "individual" right to *bear* arms can only be exercised by members of a functioning, organized state militia who bear the arms while and as a part of actively participating in the organized militia's activities. The "individual" right to keep arms only applies to members of such a militia, and then only if the federal and state governments fail to provide the firearms necessary for such militia service. At present, virtually the only such organized and actively functioning militia is the National Guard, and this has been the case for many years. Currently, the federal government provides the necessary implements of warfare, including firearms, to the National Guard, and this likewise has long been the case. Thus, under this model, the Second Amendment poses no obstacle to the wholesale disarmament of the American people. A number of our sister circuits have accepted this model, sometimes referred to by commentators as the sophisticated collective rights model. On appeal the government has abandoned the states' rights model and now advocates the sophisticated collective rights model.

The third model is simply that the Second Amendment recognizes the right of individuals to keep and bear arms. This is the view advanced by Emerson and adopted by the district court. None of our sister circuits has subscribed to this model, known by commentators as the individual rights model or the standard model. The individual rights view has enjoyed considerable academic endorsement, especially in the last two decades.

We now turn to the question of whether the district court erred in adopting an individual rights or standard model as the basis of its construction of the Second Amendment.

## Stare Decisis and United States v. Miller

The government steadfastly maintains that the Supreme Court's decision in *United States v. Miller* (1939), mandated acceptance of the collective rights or sophisticated collective rights model, and rejection of the individual rights or standard model, as a basis for construction of the Second Amendment. We disagree.

Only in *United States v. Miller* has the Supreme Court rendered any holding respecting the Second Amendment as applied to the federal government. There, the indictment charged the defendants with transporting in interstate commerce, from Oklahoma to Arkansas, an unregistered "Stevens shotgun having a barrel less than 18 inches in length" without having the required stamped written order, contrary to the National Firearms Act [1934]. The defendants filed a demurrer challenging the facial validity of the indictment on the ground that "[t]he National Firearms Act ... offends the inhibition of the Second Amendment," and "[t]he District Court held that section 11 of the Act [proscribing interstate transportation of a firearm, as therein defined, that lacked registration or a stamped order] violates the Second Amendment. It accordingly sustained the demurrer and quashed the indictment." The government appealed, and we have examined a copy of its brief. The *Miller* defendants neither filed any brief nor made any appearance in the Supreme Court.

The government's Supreme Court brief "[p]reliminarily" points out that:

> ... the National Firearms Act does not apply to all firearms but only to a limited class of firearms. The term 'firearm' is defined in Section 1 of the Act ... to refer only to 'a shotgun or rifle having a barrel of less than 18 inches in length, or any other weapon, except a pistol or revolver, from which a shot is discharged by an explosive if such weapon is capable of being concealed on the person, or a machine gun, and includes a muffler or silencer for any firearm whether or not such firearm is included within the foregoing definition.'

In this connection the brief goes on to assert that it is "indisputable that Congress was striking not at weapons intended for legitimate use but at weapons which form the arsenal of the gangster and the desperado" and that the National Firearms Act restricts interstate transportation "of only those weapons which are the tools of the criminal."

## The Government's Arguments in *Miller*

The government's brief thereafter makes essentially two legal arguments.

First, it contends that the right secured by the Second Amendment "only one which exists where the arms are borne in the militia or some other military organization provided for by law and intended for the protection of the state." This, in essence, is the sophisticated collective rights model.

The second of the government's two arguments in *Miller* is reflected by the following passage from its brief:

> While some courts have said that the right to bear arms includes the right of the individual to have them for the protection of his person and property as well as the right of the people to bear them collectively (*People v. Brown*, 253 Mich. 537; *State v. Duke*, 42 Tex. 455), the cases are unanimous in holding that the term "arms" as used in constitutional provisions refers only to those weapons which are ordinarily used for military or public defense purposes and does not relate to those weapons which are commonly used by criminals.

## The Court's Interpretation of the *Miller* Ruling and the Second Amendment

*Miller* reversed the decision of the district court and "remanded for further proceedings." We believe it is entirely clear that the Supreme Court decided *Miller* on the basis of the government's second argument—that a "shotgun having a barrel of less than eighteen inches in length" as stated in the National Firearms Act is not (or cannot merely be assumed to be) one of the "Arms" which the Second Amendment prohibits infringement of the right of the people to keep and bear—and not on the basis of the government's first argument (that the Second Amendment protects the right of the people to keep and bear no character of "arms" when not borne in actual, active service in the militia or some other military organization provided for by law). *Miller* expresses its holding as follows:

> In the absence of any evidence tending to show that possession or use of a 'shotgun having a barrel of less than eighteen inches in length' at this time has some reasonable relationship to the preservation or efficiency of a well regulated militia, we cannot say that the Second Amendment guarantees the right to keep and bear such an instrument. Certainly it is not within judicial notice that this weapon is any part of the ordinary military equipment or that its use could contribute to the common defense.

Nor do we believe that any other portion of the *Miller* opinion supports the sophisticated collective rights model. . . .

We conclude that *Miller* does not support the government's collective rights or sophisticated collective rights approach to the Second Amendment. Indeed, to the extent that *Miller* sheds light on the matter it cuts against the government's position. Nor does the government cite any other authority binding on this panel which mandates acceptance of its position in this respect. However, we do not proceed on the assumption that *Miller* actually accepted an individual rights, as opposed to a collective or sophisticated collective rights, interpretation of the Second Amendment. Thus, *Miller* itself does not resolve that issue. We turn, therefore, to an analysis of history and wording of the Second Amendment for guidance. In undertaking this analysis, we are mindful that almost all of our sister circuits have rejected any individual rights view of the Second Amendment. However, it respectfully appears to us that all or almost all of these opinions seem to have done so either on the erroneous assumption that *Miller* resolved that issue or without sufficient articulated examination of the history and text of the Second Amendment.

We begin construing the Second Amendment by examining its text: "[a] well regulated Militia, being necessary to the security of a free State, the right of the people to keep and bear Arms, shall not be infringed." U.S. Const. amend. II.

## The Meaning of "the People"

The states' rights model requires the word "people" to be read as though it were "States" or "States respectively." This would also require a corresponding change in the balance of the text to something like "to provide for the militia to keep and bear arms." That is not only far removed from the actual wording of the Second Amendment, but also would be in substantial tension with Art. 1, § 8, Cl. 16 (Congress has the power "To provide for . . . arming . . . the militia. . . ."). For the sophisticated collective rights model to be viable, the word "people" must be read as the words "members of a select militia." The individual rights model, of course, does not require that any special or unique meaning be attributed to the word "people." It gives the same meaning to the words "the people" as used in the Second Amendment phrase "the right of the people" as when used in the exact same phrase in the contemporaneously submitted and ratified First and Fourth Amendments.

There is no evidence in the text of the Second Amendment, or any other part of the Constitution, that the words "the people" have a different connotation within the Second Amendment than when employed elsewhere in the Constitution. In fact, the text of the Constitution, as a whole, strongly suggests that the words "the people" have precisely the same meaning within the Second Amendment as without. . . .

It appears clear that "the people," as used in the Constitution, including the Second Amendment, refers to individual Americans.

## The Meaning of "Bear Arms"

Proponents of the states' rights and sophisticated collective rights models argue that the phrase "bear arms" only applies to a member of the militia carrying weapons during actual militia service. Champions of the individual rights model opine that "bear arms" refers to any carrying of weapons, whether by a soldier or a civilian. There is no question that the phrase "bear arms" may be used to refer to the carrying of arms by a soldier or militiaman. The issue is whether "bear arms" was also commonly used to refer to the carrying of arms by a civilian.

[Discussion of early interpretations of the meaning of the phrase "bear arms" omitted.]

We conclude that the phrase "bear arms" refers generally to the carrying or wearing of arms. It is certainly proper to use the phrase in reference to the carrying or wearing of arms by a soldier or militiaman; thus, the context in which "bear arms" appears may indicate that it refers to a military situation, e.g. the conscientious objector clauses cited by amici supporting the government. However, amici's argument that "bear arms" was exclusively, or even usually, used to *only* refer to the carrying or wearing of arms by a soldier or militiaman must be rejected. The appearance of "bear Arms" in the Second Amendment accords fully with the plain meaning of the subject of the substantive guarantee, "the people," and offers no support for the proposition that the Second Amendment applies only during periods of actual military service or only to those who are members of a select militia. Finally, our view of "bear arms" as used in the Second Amendment appears to be the same as that expressed in the dissenting opinion of Justice [Ruth Bader] Ginsburg (joined by the Chief Justice [William H. Rehnquist] and Justices [Antonin] Scalia and [David H.] Souter) in *Muscarello v. United States* (1998); viz:

> Surely a most familiar meaning [of carrying a firearm] is, as the Constitution's Second Amendment ("keep and bear Arms") . . . and *Black's Law Dictionary*, at 214, indicate: "wear, bear, or carry . . . upon the person or in the clothing or in a pocket, for the purpose . . . of being armed and ready for offensive or defensive action in a case of conflict with another person."

## The Meaning of "Keep . . . Arms"

Neither the government nor amici argue that "keep . . . Arms" commands a military connotation. The plain meaning of the right of the people to keep arms is that it is an individual, rather than a collective, right and is not limited to keeping arms while engaged in active military service or as a member of a select militia such as the National Guard.

## The Substantive Guarantee as a Whole

Taken as a whole, the text of the Second Amendment's substantive guarantee is not suggestive of a collective rights or sophisticated collective rights interpretation, and the implausibility of either such interpretation is enhanced by consideration of the guarantee's placement within the Bill of Rights and the wording of the other articles thereof and of the original Constitution as a whole.

## The Effect of the Preamble

We turn now to the Second Amendment's preamble: "A well-regulated Militia, being necessary to the security of a free State." And, we ask ourselves whether this preamble suffices to mandate what would be an otherwise implausible collective rights or sophisticated collective rights interpretation of the amendment. We conclude that it does not.

Certainly, the preamble implies that the substantive guarantee is one which tends to enable, promote or further the existence, continuation or effectiveness of that "well-regulated Militia" which is "necessary to the security of a free State." As the Court said in *Miller*, immediately after quoting the militia clauses of Article I, § 8 (cl. 15 and 16), "[w]ith obvious purpose to assure the continuation and render possible the effectiveness of such forces the declaration and guarantee of the Second Amendment were made." We conclude that the Second Amendment's substantive guarantee, read as guaranteeing individual rights, may as so read reasonably be understood as being a guarantee which tends to enable, promote or further the existence, continuation or effectiveness of that "well-regulated Militia" which is "necessary to the security of a free State." Accordingly, the preamble does not support an interpretation of the amendment's substantive guarantee in accordance with the collective rights or sophisticated collective rights model, as such an interpretation is contrary to the plain meaning of the text of the guarantee, its placement within the Bill of Rights and the wording of the other articles thereof and of the original Constitution as a whole. . . .

## The Court Finds That the Second Amendment Protects Individual Rights Generally

We reject the collective rights and sophisticated collective rights models for interpreting the Second Amendment. We hold, consistent with *Miller*, that it protects the right of individuals, including those not then actually a member of any militia or engaged in active military service or training, to privately possess and bear their own firearms, such as the pistol involved here, that are suitable as personal, individual weapons and are not of the general kind or type excluded by *Miller*. However, because of our holding that section 922(g)(8), as applied to Emerson, does not infringe his individual rights under the Second Amendment we will not now further elaborate as to the exact scope of all Second Amendment rights.

## The Application to *Emerson*: The Right May Be Restricted

The district court held that section 922(g)(8) was unconstitutionally overbroad because it allows Second Amendment rights to be infringed absent any express judicial finding that the person subject to the order posed a future danger. In other words, the section 922(g)(8) threshold for deprivation of the fundamental right to keep and bear arms is too low.

Although, as we have held, the Second Amendment does protect individual rights, that does not mean that those rights may never be made subject to any limited, narrowly tailored specific exceptions or restrictions for particular cases that are reasonable and not inconsistent with the right of Americans generally to individually keep and bear their private arms as historically understood in this country. Indeed, Emerson does not contend, and the district court did not hold, otherwise. As we have previously noted, it is clear that felons, infants and those of unsound mind may be prohibited from possessing firearms. . . . Emerson's argument that his Second Amendment rights have been violated is grounded on the propositions that the September 14, 1998 order contains no express finding that he represents a credible threat to the physical safety of his wife (or child), that the evidence before the court issuing the order would not sustain such a finding and that the provisions of the order bringing it within clause (C)(ii) of section 922(g)(8) were no more than uncontested boiler-plate. In essence, Emerson, and the district court, concede that had the order contained an express finding, on the basis of adequate evidence, that Emerson actually posed a credible threat to the physical safety of his wife, and had that been a genuinely contested matter at the hearing, with the parties and the court aware of section 922(g)(8), then Emerson could, consistent with the Second Amendment, be precluded from possessing a firearm while he remained subject to the order.

Though we are concerned with the lack of express findings in the order, and with the absence of any requirement for same in clause (C)(ii) of section 922(g)(8), we are ultimately unpersuaded by Emerson's argument. . . .

In light of the foregoing, we cannot say that section 922(g)(8)(C)(ii)'s lack of a requirement for an explicit, express credible threat finding by the court issuing the order—of itself or together with appellate court review being available (prior to final judgment) only by mandamus—renders that section infirm under the Second Amendment. The presence of such an explicit finding would likely furnish some additional indication that the issuing court properly considered the matter, but such findings can be as much "boilerplate" or in error as any other part of such an order.

> *"Nothing in this case turns on the original meaning of the Second Amendment, so no court need follow what the majority has said in that regard."*

# Concurring Opinion: Whether the Right to Bear Arms Is an Individual or Collective Right Is of No Consequence in This Case

*Judge Robert M. Parker*

*Now-retired judge Robert M. Parker received his bachelor's and LLB degrees from the University of Texas at Austin and served in the courts for more than twenty years. Upon his fifteenth year with the U.S. District Court for the Eastern District in 1990, he was named that court's chief judge. In 1994 he was nominated by President Bill Clinton to the U.S. Court of Appeals for the Fifth Circuit, where he served until retiring in 2002.*

*In his qualified concurring opinion, Judge Robert M. Parker disagrees with the majority opinion's long analysis of and conclusions regarding the meaning of the Second Amendment. Because the court's opinion that the Second Amendment provides an individual right was not necessary or wholly relevant to this case and its outcome, the opinion is dicta—extraneous judicial remarks that do not impact the court's conclusions—not binding*

Judge Robert M. Parker, concurring opinion, *United States v. Emerson*, U.S. Fifth Circuit Court of Appeals, October 16, 2001.

*case law, and Parker wishes to clarify this. He also uses his concurring opinion to reveal facts of the case not mentioned in the majority opinion, which he argues have significant bearing on the decision.*

> Concurring Opinion: Whether the Right to Bear Arms Is an Individual or Collective Right Is of No Consequence in This Case
>
> *Judge Robert M. Parker*

I concur in the opinion except for Section V. I choose not to join Section V, which concludes that the right to keep and bear arms under the Second Amendment is an individual right, because it is dicta and is therefore not binding on us or on any other court. The determination whether the rights bestowed by the Second Amendment are collective or individual is entirely unnecessary to resolve this case and has no bearing on the judgment we dictate by this opinion. The fact that the 84 pages of dicta contained in Section V are interesting, scholarly, and well written does not change the fact that they are dicta and amount to at best an advisory treatise on this long-running debate.

## A Misplaced Debate

As federal judges it is our special charge to avoid constitutional questions when the outcome of the case does not turn on how we answer.... Furthermore, the fact that a trial court passed on a novel question of constitutional law does not require us to do likewise. Appellate courts are supposed to review judgments, not opinions.... Here, whether "the district court erred in adopting an individual rights or standard model as the basis for its construction of the Second Amendment" ... is not a question that affects the outcome of this case no matter how it is answered. In holding that § 922(g)(8) is not infirm as to Emerson, and at the same time finding an individual right to gunownership, the majority today departs from these sound precepts of judicial restraint.

No doubt the special interests and academics on both sides of this debate will take great interest in the fact that at long last some court has determined (albeit in dicta) that the Second Amendment bestows an individual right. The real issue, however, is the fact that whatever the nature or parameters of the Second Amendment right, be it collective or individual, it is a right subject to reasonable regulation. The debate, therefore, over the nature of the right is misplaced. In the final analysis, whether the right to keep and bear arms is collective or individual is of no legal consequence. It is, as duly noted by the majority opinion, a right subject to reasonable regulation. If determining that Emerson had an individual Second Amendment right that could have been successfully asserted as a defense against the charge of violating § 922(g)(8), then the issue would be cloaked with legal significance. As it stands, it makes no difference. Section 922(g)(8) is simply another example of a reasonable restriction on whatever right is contained in the Second Amendment.

And whatever the scope of the claimed Second Amendment right, no responsible individual or organization would suggest that it would protect Emerson's possession of the other guns found in his military-style arsenal the day the federal indictment was handed down. In addition to the Beretta nine millimeter pistol at issue here, Emerson had a second Beretta like the first, a semi-automatic M-1 carbine, an SKS assault rifle with bayonet, and a semi-automatic M-14 assault rifle. Nor would anyone suggest that Emerson's claimed right to keep and bear arms supersedes that of his wife, their daughter, and of others to be free from bodily harm or threats of harm. Though I see no mention of it in the majority's opinion, the evidence shows that Emerson pointed the Beretta at his wife and daughter when the two went to his office to retrieve an insurance payment. When his wife moved to retrieve her shoes, Emerson cocked the hammer and made ready to fire. Emerson's instability and threatening conduct also manifested itself in comments to his office staff and the police. Emerson told an employee that he had an AK-47 and in the same breath that he planned to pay a visit to his wife's boyfriend. To a police officer he said that if any of his wife's friends were to set foot on his property they would "be found dead in the parking lot."

If the majority was only filling the *Federal Reporter* with page after page of non-binding dicta there would be no need for me to write separately. As I have said, nothing in this case turns on the original meaning of the Second Amendment, so no court need follow what the majority has said in that regard. Unfortunately, however, the majority's exposition pertains to one of the most hotly-contested issues of the day. By overreaching in the area of Second Amendment law, the majority stirs this controversy without necessity when prudence and respect for *stare decisis* calls for it to say nothing at all. . . . Indeed, in the end, the majority today may have done more harm than good for those who embrace a right to gunownership.

*"A more productive debate ... would focus less on how the [Second Amendment] provision was understood in 1791 and more on how the United States has changed since then."*

# The Limits Placed on Gun Control

*Michael C. Dorf*

*Michael C. Dorf, Harvard graduate and the Isidor & Seville Sulzbacher professor of law at Columbia University School of Law, has been a professor at Columbia since 1995, before which time he taught at Rutgers University and clerked for U.S. Supreme Court Justice Anthony M. Kennedy and Judge Stephen Reinhardt of the U.S. Court of Appeals, Ninth Circuit. He is widely published in law journals, and among his book credits are* On Reading the Constitution, *which he coauthored with Laurence H. Tribe, and* No Litmus Test Law and Politics in the Twenty-First Century, *published in 2006.*

*In this discussion of* United States v. Emerson *and the issues surrounding the case, Michael C. Dorf notes that much of the* Emerson *reading of the Second Amendment is logical and understandable—but that it is flawed as well. He argues that some of the court's conclusions, even if grounded in logic, present disturbing consequent scenarios and that the collective-rights interpretation is just as valid. Continuing, Dorf points out a relevant case more recent than the oft-cited* United States v. Miller *and*

Michael C. Dorf, "Federal Court of Appeals Says the Second Amendment Places Limits on Gun Control Legislation," *Findlaw: Legal News and Commentary*, October 31, 2001. Copyright © 1994-2007 FindLaw. Reproduced by permission.

*furthermore questions the Fifth Circuit's interpretation of the writers' circumstances, understandings, and language at the time of the amendment's composition. Ultimately, Dorf points out the problems in looking at the Second Amendment in the context only of the eighteenth century, when many relevant circumstances and factors are vastly different in the twenty-first.*

The debate over gun control in the United States is primarily a debate over policy. For many years, however, gun rights advocates have tried to invoke the Constitution as a trump card. The question whether guns should be legal, they say, should not be about aggregate costs and benefits because Second Amendment settles the issue in favor of gun rights.

The Second Amendment argument has generally received a cool reception in the courts. Former Chief Justice of the United States Warren Burger even went so far as to label it a "fraud on the American public."

Now, however, for the first time, a federal appeals court has come down squarely on the side of those who argue that the Second Amendment right to keep and bear arms restricts the government's authority to enact gun control legislation.

Although the court's opinion permits some limits on firearms possession and use—such as laws forbidding ex-felons to carry guns or prohibiting guns on airplanes—it places the burden of justifying these limits on the government. That marks a substantial change from the prior attitude of judicial deference to gun control legislation.

## The *Emerson* Case

The ruling in question is *United States v. Emerson* [2001], issued by the U.S. Court of Appeals for the Fifth Circuit. *Emerson* endorsed what the court called the "individual rights model" of the Second Amendment.

The *Emerson* case originally arose from state court divorce proceedings. In 1998, Dr. Timothy Emerson was ordered by a

Texas judge not to threaten or harm his daughter or his estranged wife. (Emerson's ex-wife had testified that he had previously threatened to kill a friend of hers.)

A federal statue makes it a crime for a person under such an order to possess a firearm, provided that the firearm affects or has moved in interstate commerce. Shortly after the order was issued, Emerson was indicted by a federal grand jury for possessing a firearm in violation of the statute.

Emerson challenged his indictment on a number of grounds, including the Second Amendment. The federal district court dismissed the indictment. On appeal, the Fifth Circuit reversed, upholding the indictment, because it found that the government had advanced a compelling reason for overriding Emerson's Second Amendment rights.

The court's result meant that it did not really have to reach the question of whether Emerson had Second Amendment rights in the first place. After all, even assuming he did, the court had found the government's interest overrode them. Nonetheless, a majority of the three-judge panel devoted the bulk of its opinion to interpreting the Second Amendment.

Because the majority did not have to reach the Second Amendment question, its analysis technically constitutes what lawyers call dicta—that is, reasoning unnecessary to the disposition of a case. Nevertheless, the majority's opinion could have a substantial impact on the future of gun control in the United States because other courts may follow its reasoning.

## Three Second Amendment Models

The Second Amendment states: "A well regulated Militia, being necessary to the security of a free State, the right of the people to keep and bear arms, shall not be infringed."

The appeals court majority identified three "models" of the Second Amendment. The first and second both emphasize the preamble, or "purpose" clause, of the Amendment—the words "A well regulated Militia, being necessary to the security of a free State." The third does not.

The first model holds that the right to keep and bear arms belongs to the people collectively rather than to individuals, because the right's only purpose is to enable states to maintain a militia; it is not for individuals' benefit.

The second model is similar to the first. It holds that the right to keep and bear arms exists only for individuals actively serving in the militia, and then only pursuant to such regulations as may be prescribed.

Under either of the first two models, a private citizen has no right to possess a firearm for personal use. But the court rejected these two models in favor of a third, the individual rights model.

Under this third model, the Second Amendment protects a right of individuals to own and possess firearms, much as the First Amendment protects a right of individuals to engage in free speech.

## A Key Early Second Amendment Precedent

In endorsing the third, individual rights model, the Fifth Circuit broke ranks with the other federal appeals courts that have addressed the issue, all of which have adopted some variant of the first two models. In a sense, the Fifth Circuit was entitled to differ: Decisions of one circuit court are not binding on other circuit courts, and a Circuit split can always be resolved by the Supreme Court.

But did the Fifth Circuit's analysis violate Supreme Court precedent? That is an issue of greater moment, for Supreme Court precedent is, of course, binding upon the federal courts of appeals.

One important Second Amendment precedent is the 1939 decision of *United States v. Miller*. There, the Supreme Court rejected a Second Amendment challenge to an indictment for possession of a sawed-off shotgun in violation of federal law.

In a terse opinion, the Court concluded: "In the absence of any evidence tending to show that possession or use of a [sawed-off shotgun] at this time has some reasonable relationship to the preservation or efficiency of a well regulated militia, we cannot say that the Second Amendment guarantees the right to keep and bear such an instrument. Certainly it is not within judicial notice that this weapon is any part of the ordinary military equipment or that its use could contribute to the common defense."

Host courts and many commentators have read *Miller* as officially adopting the collective right view of the Second Amendment—that is, one of the views set forth in the first or second model that the Fifth Circuit described in its opinion. However, in *Emerson*, the Fifth Circuit rejected that reading of *Miller*.

Based on a re-examination of the government's brief in *Miller* and the language just quoted, the Fifth Circuit concluded that *Miller* can at least as easily be read to stand for the opposite conclusion: that *if a weapon were of the sort that could be used by the military, there would be an individual right to possess that weapon*. Thus, a sawed-off shotgun, because it is not a military weapon, falls outside the Second Amendment—but a more "military" weapon would not.

This is a plausible reading of *Miller*'s language, but it has extraordinarily perverse consequences. It would seem to grant the most constitutional protection to just those weapons that are least suitable to private possession, and least likely to be geared toward personal protection alone: distinctly military "arms" such as tanks, attack helicopters, rocket launchers, or even nuclear missiles.

## A More Recent Second Amendment Precedent

Perhaps in recognition of this oddity, the Fifth Circuit did not affirmatively rely on *Miller*, instead only going so far as to say that *Miller* is not controlling in either direction. But whether even that more limited conclusion is justified is itself subject to doubt, because Supreme Court cases since *Miller* have read the case as endorsing something like the collective right view.

For example, in a 1980 case, *Lewis v. United States*, the Court upheld a federal statute prohibiting a convicted felon from possessing firearms. The *Lewis* Court cited *Miller* for the proposition that the statute at issue did not "trench upon any constitutionally protected liberties." Significantly, the statute at issue in *Lewis* applied to *all* firearms—not just "unmilitary" ones like a sawed-off shotgun. If military-type weapons triggered Second Amendment rights, presumably the Court would have said so in *Lewis*.

Perhaps the *Lewis* case is a misreading of *Miller*, but if so, it is a misreading by the U.S. Supreme Court itself, whose decisions and language are supposed to bind federal appeals courts.

## Text and Original Understanding: The Bill of Individual Rights?

Treating the *Emerson* case as presenting a question of first impression, the Fifth Circuit opted for the third, individual rights model because it found that approach most consistent with the text and history of the Second Amendment.

The Fifth Circuit opinion makes a plausible case for this view. However, the arguments are more balanced than the court acknowledged. Let us consider a few key points.

The Fifth Circuit placed considerable reliance on the text surrounding the Second Amendment. The Amendment sits squarely inside the Bill of Rights, which generally protects individual rights. Moreover, the Amendment protects a right of "the people"—and when that term is used elsewhere in the Constitution, it refers to the people in their individual rather than their collective capacity. Accordingly, the Fifth Circuit thought the Second Amendment also protects an individual right.

## Preambles and Purpose

Yet, if one is to look at adjacent text, surely one should start with text that appears within the Second Amendment itself. That takes us to the Second Amendment's arresting preamble, which sets for the amendment's purpose: "A well regulated Militia, being necessary to the security of a free State. . . ."

Only one other operative provision of the Constitution contains anything resembling this. Article I, Section 8, Clause 8 gives Congress the power "to promote the Progress of Science and useful Arts, by securing for limited Times to Authors and Inventors the exclusive Right to their respective Writings and Discoveries." This, of course, is the clause authorizing copyrights and patents.

A preamble invites interpreters to construe the operative text in light of the purposes set forth in the preamble. Yet that is not how the Fifth Circuit proceeded.

The Fifth Circuit read the language "keep and bear arms" to refer to individual possession and use of arms. If the "keep and bear" language stood alone, that would be a perfectly appropriate reading. However, once we have been alerted by the Second Amendment's preamble to the fact that the provision has something to do with militias, we may be open to other readings.

## Founding Era Documents

Moreover, if one reads Founding Era documents, one finds that the phrase "bear arms" was almost always used to refer to military service. (The interested reader can try this himself or herself by searching for the phrase "bear arms" in the Library of Congress's database of congressional and other documents from the founding era.)

To be sure, one can find the occasional usage suggesting the right is not always related to military service—especially among Pennsylvanians. For example, the Pennsylvania Constitution of 1776 provided, in part: "The people have a right to bear arms for the defense of themselves and the State." Furthermore, as the Fifth Circuit noted, some Pennsylvania Antifederalists would have gone even further, proposing an amendment that stated, in part, "That the people have a right to bear arms for the defence of themselves and their own State, or the United States, or for the purpose of killing game."

Yet while these uses show that the phrase "bear arms" could be, and sometimes was, adapted to include activities outside of the organized military, they hardly cast doubt on the dominant Founding Era usage.

What about the fact that the Second Amendment protects not merely the right to "bear" but also to "keep" arms? The Fifth Circuit thought that "keep" certainly means "possess." But that is not necessarily correct.

At the Founding, "keep and bear" appears to have been understood as a unitary phrase, like other constitutional terms such as "cruel and unusual" or "necessary and proper." In my own research, I have not come across any documents of the Founding period that treat "keep" as adding a right to private possession distinct from the military notion of arms-bearing.

## The Second Amendment in the Twenty-First Century

By making these arguments, I do not mean to suggest that the Fifth Circuit's decision reflects bad historical research. Overall, *Emerson* is a scholarly opinion that makes a plausible argument. My point, instead, is that a plausible (and in my own view somewhat more convincing) historical case can also be made for something like the collective right model of the Second Amendment.

With plausible historical arguments on both sides, and ambiguous text, what should courts do? Should they convene a panel of eminent historians to decide what the Second Amendment *really* meant in 1791? That would hardly settle the matter because historians are nearly as quarrelsome a lot as lawyers.

A more productive debate over the Second Amendment's meaning would focus less on how the provision was understood in 1791 and more on how the United States has changed since then.

Consider just one such change: the fact that professional police forces as we know them today were first created in the nineteenth century—long after the Second Amendment was penned and made supreme law. Prior to the emergence of the police, ordinary citizens would bring what arms they had in response to a "hue and cry" or when serving on a posse comitatus. (Think of a sheriff in the old west rounding up a "posse" to bring an outlaw to justice.)

If private firearm ownership served as a means of collective self-defense, does the assumption of that function by professionals render the Second Amendment obsolete? Or is the Second Amendment only obsolete in those places where police are effective?

Put another way, do citizens living in high-crime neighborhoods that receive inadequate police services retain a residual right of armed self-defense? Would they still have such a right even if it turned out that they were, in fact, actually subject to greater danger armed than unarmed?

These are not easy questions to answer, but they are only made more difficult by the pretense that we can find the answers if only we look deeply enough into the Eighteenth Century. How to interpret the Second Amendment in the Twenty-First Century is a question that only Twenty-First Century Americans can answer.

"*In* United States v. Emerson, *the United States Court of Appeals for the Fifth Circuit re-energized popular debate about the meaning of the Second Amendment.*"

# The Fifth Circuit Disregarded Contemporary Issues, Focusing Solely on the 1789 Constitutional Text

*Akhil and Vikram Amar*

*The Amar brothers write a regular column in* Writ, *an online legal resource, and have also contributed to the* New York Times, Los Angeles Times, *and* Washington Post. *Publishing together and separately, they have written four books and numerous scholarly essays. Akhil graduated from Yale College and Yale Law School, where he currently teaches. Vikram graduated from the University of California at Berkeley and Yale Law School. He teaches at the University of California Hastings College of Law.*

*In the following selection, Akhil and Vikram Amar probe the constitutionality of the* Emerson *opinion, explicitly investigating the language in the Second Amendment to support the collective-right argument. Additionally, they explore how other amendments have influenced the modern interpretation of the Second Amendment's importance. They determine that the court nar-*

*rowly interpreted the Constitution in its 1789 historical context, ignoring subsequent amendments that provide a sense of equality, and therefore more legitimately reflect the spirit of the Constitution.*

A federal appellate panel ruled last week [October 2001] that the Constitution guarantees a limited right of individual Americans to keep guns for nonmilitary purposes. By so ruling in *United States v. Emerson*, the United States Court of Appeals for the Fifth Circuit re-energized popular debate about the meaning of the Second Amendment and also created a split among federal appellate courts, thus increasing the odds that the Supreme Court will soon weigh in with its own reading of the Amendment.

Citizens who enter the fray—be they Justices or other judges, lawyers or layfolk—should be wary of the Fifth Circuit's opinion. Though the Circuit may have reached the right conclusion, both in recognizing an individual right and in deeming it nonabsolute, the court told the wrong constitutional story.

And make no mistake, the story Americans tell themselves about liberty matters, and the story judges tell us especially matters, for these are the stories that shape our self-image and ultimately determine who has rights, to what, and why.

## The *Emerson* Opinion and the Constitution

As our fellow *Writ* columnist Michael Dorf has explained more fully, *Emerson* involved a man who brandished a firearm against his estranged wife in violation of a federal statute. Parting company with other federal courts, which have limited the application of the Second Amendment to organized militias like the National Guard, the Fifth Circuit insisted that the amendment affirms a broader individual right to own guns. The court also ruled that this right must yield to reasonable regulations, including the gun statute at issue.

Professor Dorf and other commentators have thoughtfully discussed whether the *Emerson* ruling is consistent with current Supreme Court precedent. But as United States Chief Justice John Marshall observed over 150 years ago, "it is a Constitution"—and not the U.S. Reports, which compile judicial opinions—that "we are expounding." And when we turn to the Constitution itself, we see that the Fifth Circuit's account of the document is lacking.

The Fifth Circuit claimed that the Second Amendment's text and history compel an individual rights reading. But they do not.

## The Meaning of the Phrase "Bear Arms"

Indeed, the *Emerson* court found only one clear nonmilitary use of the phrase before 1789. Against this linguistic outlier are scores of military allusions to arms-bearing in eighteenth-century laws and legal sources.

The Second Amendment's overall context further strengthens the military reading of the phrase "bear arms." The Amendment speaks of a "militia"—another military term—and flanks the Third Amendment, which addresses the military issue of troop quartering. Most eighteenth-century state constitutions likewise linked arms-bearing to other military matters.

## Evidence for a Collective, Not an Individual, Right

Moreover, in considering whether the Second Amendment creates an individual or a collective right, we should note that the Amendment speaks of a collective "people," not individual "persons."

Elsewhere, the Constitution most often uses "the people" as a collective noun embodying voters and jurors, rather than all citizens. The Preamble, for example, states that "We, the people"—that is, voters—ordained and established the Constitution. Similarly, Article I directs that the House of Representatives shall be elected biannually by "the people"—once again, voters.

And of course, at the Founding the class of voters was very different from the class of citizens. Women, children, and aliens fell outside this core definition of voting "people." They were likewise excluded from the Second Amendment's "militia."

The Second Amendment's syntax, too, suggests that the "militia" and the "people" are, roughly speaking, synonymous; the use of "people" in the Amendment's second clause in effect refers back to the use of "militia" in its introductory clause. (Indeed, an early draft spoke explicitly of the militia "composed of the body of the people." The final draft makes this point with fewer words.)

According to the Amendment's basic vision, all voters ideally should serve in the military, and the military in turn should be composed of ordinary voters. This conception is quite far afield from today's professional military. However, it can be more easily understood by thinking of the early military as somewhat similar to a jury, another local collectivist institution closely akin to the militia. At the founding, one would have not only a jury of one's peers, but ideally a militia of one's peers as well.

## The Historical, and the Contemporary, Second Amendment

None of this means that *Emerson* is wrong in result or that the Constitution cannot now be read to protect a qualified individual right to possess guns outside the military. Other constitutional clauses are read nonliterally and the Second Amendment may likewise be read expansively.

Law and language have evolved; today it is common to speak of nonmilitary arms-bearing. Many modern state constitutions embrace a limited right of individual gun ownership, and millions of Americans deem guns a fundamental right, though not an absolute one. The fact that there are almost as many firearms as citizens in this country similarly suggests that, like it or not, guns are part of the American ethos.

## How Later Amendments May Have Altered the Second Amendment's Meaning

Most importantly, we must remember that our Constitution differs dramatically from the Framers'. Over the centuries, We the People have made amends for some of the Founding fathers' failures. And some of these amendments speak to the question of who in America should be trusted with arms.

The great generation that won the Civil War had a more individualistic view of liberty than did the Founders, and this later generation's Fourteenth Amendment, adopted in 1868, reflected that individualistic worldview. Concretely, the Amendment pledged to protect various fundamental "privileges and immunities" of individuals.

One such "privilege" explicitly embraced by the Reconstruction Congress in legislation accompanying the Fourteenth Amendment was a limited right to have a gun in one's home for self-protection, because police in the 1860s could not always be trusted to protect blacks from white nightriders and other thugs. This right to a gun was seen as a right of all citizens—women as well as men, blacks as well as whites—even if the gun owner was not a voter or militiaman.

The Fourteenth Amendment, which *Emerson* virtually ignored, both anchors an individual right in constitutional text and explains why this right is properly limited by other rights, like the right to be free from irresponsible gun use and thuggery.

Instead of detailing the Fourteenth Amendment's new birth of freedom—and the way it might alter our understanding of the Second Amendment—*Emerson* blandly cited parts of the Supreme Court's infamous 1857 *Dred Scott* case, without even noting that much of that case was repudiated by the Fourteenth Amendment. (*Dred Scott* held that blacks, even if free, could never be citizens, and were entitled to little respect from whites. The Fourteenth Amendment explicitly overruled this holding by promising citizenship to all born in America— rich and poor, black and white, male and female—and by further promising to protect all citizens in their fundamental "privileges and immunities.")

Nor did America's constitutional saga end with the Fourteenth Amendment. In 1870, the Fifteenth Amendment enfranchised black men because they had helped win the Civil War on the battlefield—preserving the Founding linkage between military arms-bearing and voting, but extending the definition of "the people" to include former slaves and other free blacks.

## Rallying Around the Amended Constitution—Not Just the 1789 Text

*Emerson* erred by failing to weave any of these amendments into its arms-bearing story. By inflating the Founding, *Emerson* exaggerated a 1789 text adopted with little input from women and blacks. It also slighted later amendments expanding democracy, amendments that affirmed rights of previously excluded persons and included these persons in the constitutional conversation itself.

In general *Emerson's* methodological skew—that is, its exclusive focus on the founding—tends to tilt constitutional adjudication sharply rightward. Consider, for example, civil rights more generally. Unlike *Emerson*, the Warren Court understood the importance of Reconstruction and upheld every federal civil rights law it reviewed. In contrast, the Rehnquist Court, a la *Emerson*, has trivialized Reconstruction. In the name of Founding-era states' rights, the Justices have invalidated key Reconstruction-style civil rights laws protecting women, the elderly, the religious, and the disabled. The judiciary has also endorsed sex discrimination in the military and age discrimination in jury selection—types of discrimination much easier to justify if we look only to the Founders while ignoring the equality vision underlying the Fourteenth, Nineteenth, and Twenty-sixth Amendments.

With Americans under attack, our Constitution can be a rallying point uniting citizens of diverse ethnicities, faiths, and ideologies. But the document contains much more than the Founding vision. It also reflects the spirit of antislavery idealists, progressive era reformers, and 1960's activists.

When other courts and commentators revisit the gun issue, they should tell the full story, rather than merely the opening chapter, of American liberty.

> "*[The Amars'] creative insights [about the Second Amendment]. . . provoke us to reexamine our premises. . . . However, portions rely on a skewed analysis of the constitutional text.*"

# The Court Did Not Err in Its Analysis

## Stephen P. Halbrook

*Stephen P. Halbrook has been practicing civil litigation and criminal defense since receiving his Juris Doctor from Georgetown University Law Center in 1978. With a PhD in philosophy, he has also taught at several universities. Among his published books are* Firearms Law Deskbook: Federal and State Criminal Practice *(2005);* Freedmen, the Fourteenth Amendment and the Right to Bear Arms, 1866–1876 *(1998); and* Target Switzerland: Swiss Armed Neutrality in World War II *(1998).*

*Responding to the commentary by brothers Akhil and Vikram Amar, Stephen P. Halbrook here examines the Amars' historical interpretations and their criticisms of the* Emerson *ruling. Halbrook disputes some of the facts set forth by the Amars, in addition to taking a different stance with regard to the meanings of such important Second Amendment terms as "the people" and "bear arms." He finds that "the militia" and "the people" did indeed refer to different entities and also counters that the* Emerson *court should not be criticized for the ways it did, or did not, address the Fourteenth Amendment or other cases in its analysis—because, he argues, such explorations would have been beyond the scope of the case before the court.*

Stephen P. Halbrook, "*Emerson's* Second Amendment," *StephenHalbrook.com*, 2001. Reproduced by permission of the author.

In [their article] "Guns and the Constitution" [2001], Akhil and Vikram Amar offer creative insights about the right to keep and bear arms that provoke us to reexamine our premises. Much of the thesis is valid. However, portions rely on a skewed analysis of the constitutional text, and its tone is unduly harsh on the historical analysis set forth by the U.S. Court of Appeals in *United States v. Emerson.*

The Amars suggest that *Emerson* reached the right conclusion "in recognizing an individual right and in deeming it nonabsolute," but "the court told the wrong constitutional story." While they persuasively show that the story is bigger, it is worth noting that the story has not been told at all before by any other of the courts of appeals. Most are still in Second Amendment denial.

## Examining the Facts

First, let's get the facts straight. The defendant was not charged with "brandish[ing] a firearm against his estranged wife in violation of a federal statute." The federal charge is that he possessed a firearm after a domestic restraining order was entered against him. There was a separate state prosecution for brandishing, of which the jury acquitted Dr. Emerson.

We are told that the Second Amendment does not compel an individual rights reading. To "bear arms" refers to military service, not carrying guns merely for hunting or sport. "The *Emerson* court found only one clear nonmilitary use of the phrase before 1789." Not so. The Pennsylvania Declaration of Rights (1776) recognized "that the people have a right to bear arms for the defence of themselves and the state." Vermont repeated this language. This included the right, wrote James Wilson, "to keep arms for the preservation . . . of their own persons."

Jefferson drafted a bill which Madison proposed to the Virginia legislature in 1785 punishing a game-law violator if he should "bear a gun out of his inclosed ground, unless whilst performing military duty." The Minority in the Pennsylvania convention of 1788 declared "that the people have a right to bear arms for the defense of themselves . . . or for the purpose of killing game. . . ." To "bear arms" simply means to carry arms.

And what about the separate right to "keep" arms, which no one has asserted is a military term? Samuel Adams proposed in the Massachusetts convention "that the said Constitution be never construed to authorize Congress . . . to prevent the people of the United States, who are peaceable citizens, from keeping their own arms. . . ."

The facts that "militia" is a military term and that the Amendment "flanks the Third Amendment," which concerns troop quartering, mean little. It also flanks the First Amendment. Moreover, the text meticulously refers to the "militia" in certain parts and to "the people" in others. Indeed, the Fifth Amendment provides for indictment by a grand jury except in cases arising, *inter alia*, "in the militia, when in actual service in time of war or public danger."

## The Meaning of "the People"

Which brings us to the Amars' thesis that "the Amendment speaks of a collective 'people,' not individual 'persons.'" It seems that "the people" means "voters and jurors, rather than all citizens." True, the Preamble refers to "We, the people," but the voters did not "ordain and establish" the Constitution, "the conventions of nine States" did, as Article VII notes. And while Article I provides that the members of the House of Representatives shall consist of "members chosen every second year by the people of the several States," the fact that the States set qualifications for voting did not constrict the meaning of "the people" in the Bill of Rights.

The First, Second, and Fourth Amendments refer to "the right of the people" "peaceably to assemble," "to keep and bear arms," and "to be secure . . . from unreasonable searches and seizures." The Amars confuse "rights," which only individuals exercise, with "powers," meaning governmental functions. In referring to the "powers . . . reserved to the States respectively, or to the people," the Tenth Amendment means exercises of authority. These powers include—as Akhil Amar has written elsewhere—the ballot box, the jury box, and the cartridge box (the militia).

At the Founding, the Amars state, "women, children, and aliens fell outside this core definition of voting 'people.'" But this was true only of the "powers" exercised by the people, such as suffrage, the jury, and the militia. No one denied that women were among "the people" who had "the right" to keep arms or to be secure in their houses from unreasonable searches.

Nor does the syntax of the Second Amendment suggest that the "militia" and the "people" are "roughly speaking, synonymous." While the Framers favored a militia "composed of the body of the people," the fact that "militia" and "the people" were used in a single sentence precludes an interpretation that the terms are redundant. It is the "right" of individuals to have arms that encourages and provides a reservoir for the "power" of a well regulated militia.

## The Reasons for Arming

The Amars are on target in averring that, according to the Founders' vision, voters would serve in the militia, and that both juries and the militia would consist of one's peers. But it is a false dichotomy to suggest that the Amendment "confers a collective military right rather than an individual nonmilitary one." The Amars state: "The Founders were thinking of local militiamen, like those who fought at Lexington and Concord—not of hunters or sportsmen." But through hunting and target shooting, those militiamen honed their shooting skills.

In the words of Lt. Frederick MacKenzie, one of the Redcoats routed at Concord: "These fellows were generally good marksmen, and many of them used long arms made for Duckshooting." Concord militia Colonel James Barrett's 15-year-old granddaughter Meliscent told a British officer that the colonists could resist because "they would use powder horns and bullets—just as they shot bear."

While the serious federal purpose declared is "the security of a free state," not sport, this security is also protected in part by individuals who arm themselves to resist violent crime. In debates on the 1792 Militia Act, Roger Sherman "conceived it to be the privilege of every citizen, and one of his most essential rights, to bear arms, and to resist every attack upon his liberty or property, by whomsoever made." The States, "like private citizens, have a right to be armed, and to defend" themselves.

The Amars detail the expansion of rights won by the Reconstruction Amendments. They mention legislation accompanying the Fourteenth Amendment recognizing the right of all, blacks as well as whites, to be armed in one's home for self protection. This was the Freedmen's Bureau Act of 1866, which declared that all citizens shall have the "full and equal benefit of all laws and proceedings concerning personal liberty, personal security, and . . . estate, real and personal, including the constitutional right to bear arms."

## The *Emerson* Case

The Amars fault *Emerson* for ignoring the Fourteenth Amendment, the tinted glasses through which we view the Bill of Rights today. However, *Emerson* does quote Senator Howard's speech introducing the Fourteenth Amendment, whose privileges-and-immunities clause protected "the personal rights guarantied and secured by the first eight amendments of the Constitution; such as. . . the right to keep and to bear arms. . . ." *Emerson* also quotes recent Supreme Court opinions on the Fourteenth Amendment which position the Second Amendment in an equal status with the other provisions of the Bill of Rights.

*Emerson* is also faulted because it "blandly cited parts of the Supreme Court's infamous 1857 Dred Scott case" without noting that it was overruled by the Fourteenth Amendment. Yet *Scott* [*Scott v. Stanford*] was cited with other Supreme Court cases to indicate that court's mention of the Second Amendment as a right of "the people." *Emerson* refers to the page asserting that citizenship would give blacks free speech and the right "to keep and carry arms wherever they went."

*Emerson* does not involve State action and thus could not be expected to include a full blown analysis of the Fourteenth Amendment. The proper relation between military service and the later Amendments expanding voting rights to blacks, women, and 18-year olds raise intriguing philosophical questions. But one could hardly expect a court of appeals to engage in such speculations in order to decide whether a prohibition on possession of a firearm while under a domestic restraining order violates the Second Amendment.

# Organizations to Contact

*The editors have compiled the following list of organizations concerned with the issues debated in this book. The descriptions are derived from materials provided by the organizations. All have publications or information available for interested readers. The list was compiled on the date of publication of the present volume; the information provided here may change. Be aware that many organizations take several weeks or longer to respond to inquiries, so allow as much time as possible.*

**The Brady Center to Prevent Gun Violence**
1225 I St. NW, Suite 1100, Washington, DC   20005
(202) 289-7319 • fax: (202) 408-1851
Web site: www.bradycenter.org

The Brady Center is the largest national, nonpartisan, grass-roots organization leading the fight to prevent gun violence. Through the Brady Campaign and its network of Million Mom March chapters, this group rallies for sensible gun laws, regulations, and public policies and works to educate the public about gun violence. Its Web site features a substantial number of fact sheets and reports about U.S. gun-related laws, issues, politics, deaths, and injuries.

**The Coalition to Stop Gun Violence (CSGV)**
1023 15th St. NW, Suite 305, Washington, DC   20005
(202) 408-0061
Web site: www.csgv.org

Made up of forty-five national organizations, including religious organizations, child welfare advocates, public health professionals, and social justice groups, the CSGV works to reduce gun violence through various means. It is joined in its mission by the Educational Fund to Stop Gun Violence. The CSGV pushes a progressive agenda to reduce firearm death and injury, and aims to defeat the gun lobby through a strategy that encompasses legislation, litigation, and grassroots efforts. Its Web site offers information on illegal gun markets, the international arms trade, and the subject of guns and democracy.

## Gun Owners of America (GOA)

8001 Forbes Pl., Suite 102, Springfield, VA   22151
(703) 321-8585 • fax: (703) 321-8408
e-mail: goamail@gunowners.org
Web site: www.gunowners.org

The group Gun Owners of America lobbies to preserve and defend the Second Amendment rights of gun owners. The GOA sees firearms ownership as a freedom issue, and represents the views of gun owners whenever the right to bear arms is threatened on a local, state, or national level. The GOA Web site includes current and previous issues of its newsletter, *The Gun Owners.*

## The International Action Network on Small Arms (IANSA)

56–64, Leonard St., London   EC2A 4JX
    England
+44 (207) 065-0870 • fax: +44 (207) 065-0871
e-mail: contact@iansa.org
Web site: www.iansa.org

The International Action Network on Small Arms is a network of 700 civil society organizations working in 100 countries to stop the proliferation and misuse of small arms and light weapons (SALW). IANSA seeks to make people safer from gun violence by securing stronger regulation on guns in society and better controls on arms exports. IANSA is composed of a wide range of organizations concerned with small arms, including policy development organizations, national gun control groups, research institutes, aid agencies, faith groups, victims, human rights, and community action organizations. Its Web site provides a variety of resources and fact sheets on gun violence.

**National Rifle Association (NRA)**
11250 Waples Mill Rd., Fairfax, VA   22030
(800) 672-3888
Web site: www.nra.org

The NRA is a powerful pro-gun rights group in the United States. It offers shooting, training, educational, and public service programs in an effort to foster the safe and responsible ownership and use of firearms. Its Web site features various articles and links supportive of gun rights as well as information regarding gun-safety programs and training opportunities. The NRA also provides information on firearm-related legislation and politics. Among its publications are the journals *American Rifleman, American Hunter,* and *America's 1st Freedom.*

**Project Safe Neighborhoods**
U.S. Department of Justice, Washington, DC   20530-0001
(202) 514-2000
e-mail: AskPSN@usdoj.gov
Web site: www.psn.gov

Created in May 2001, Project Safe Neighborhoods links together federal, state, and local law enforcement, prosecutors, and community leaders to enact a multifaceted approach to deterring and punishing gun crime. It represents a nationwide program run by the U.S. Department of Justice, and comprises a network of existing local programs that target gun crime. The Project Safe Neighborhoods program provides funding and additional tools to support these organizations and their endeavors. Its Web site presents guides and case studies on such topics as background checks, gang-related violence, and gun-safety initiatives.

**Second Amendment Committee**
PO Box 1776, Hanford, CA   93232
(559) 584-5209 • fax: (559) 584-4084
e-mail: liberty89@libertygunrights.com
Web site: www.libertygunrights.com

The Second Amendment Committee, founded by a longtime gun-rights activist, is a nationwide organization that provides information to those seeking a peaceful resolution to the gun crisis. The committee supports the role of citizen militias, and its founder has authored legislation promoting state enforcement of the Second Amendment. The organization's Web site, which includes a blog on gun rights, reports that "many gun owners have acclaimed the Second Amendment Committee to be the *No. 1* gun defender in the nation."

## Second Amendment Foundation (SAF)
12500 NE 10th Place, Bellevue, WA   98005
(425) 454-7012 • fax: (425) 451-3959
e-mail: AdminForWeb@saf.org
Web site: www.saf.org

The Second Amendment Foundation is dedicated to promoting a better understanding of the right to privately own and possess firearms. It conducts many educational and legal-action programs designed to better inform the public about the gun-control debate. The foundation's Web site features gun-rights resources and a list of sponsored publications, including the periodical *Gun Week*.

## Stop Handgun Violence
One Bridge St. Suite 300, Newton, MA   02458
(877) SAFE ARMS • fax: (617) 965-7308
e-mail: shv@meredithmanagement.com
Web site: www.stophandgunviolence.com

Stop Handgun Violence is a nonprofit organization committed to the prevention of gun violence through education, public awareness, effective law enforcement, and common-sense gun laws—without banning guns. SHV has distributed over thirty thousand trigger locks to gun owners across the country, and has worked to establish gun-violence prevention curriculums in schools across the state of Massachusetts. The group's Web site includes stories about children and guns, gun-violence prevention tips, and information about gun laws.

**Violence Policy Center (VPC)**
1140 19th St. NW, Suite 600, Washington, DC   20036
(202) 822-8200 • fax: (202) 822-8205
e-mail: info@vpc.org
Web site: www.vpc.org

The Violence Policy Center is a national nonprofit educational foundation that conducts research on violence in America and works to develop violence-reduction policies and proposals. The Center examines the role of firearms in America, conducts research on firearms violence, and explores new ways to decrease firearm-related death and injury. The VPC releases studies on a range of gun-violence issues, including analysis of homicide data and gun law effectiveness.

# For Further Research

## Books

Amnesty International, *The Impact of Guns on Women's Lives*. London: Amnesty International, 2005.

Carl T. Bogus, ed. *The Second Amendment in Law and History: Historians and Constitutional Scholars on the Right to Bear Arms*. New York: New Press, 2000.

Laura Browder, *Her Best Shot: Women and Guns in America*. Chapel Hill: University of North Carolina Press, 2006.

Joan Burbick, *Gun Show Nation: Gun Culture and American Democracy*. New York: New Press, 2006.

Gregg Lee Carter, *Gun Control in the United States: A Reference Handbook*. Santa Barbara, CA: ABC-CLIO, 2006.

Gregg Lee Carter, ed. *Guns in American Society: An Encyclopedia of History, Politics, Culture, and the Law*. Santa Barbara, CA: ABC-CLIO, 2002.

Saul Cornell, *A Well-Regulated Militia: The Founding Fathers and the Origins of Gun Control in America*. Oxford, UK: Oxford University Press, 2006.

Constance Emerson Crooker, *Gun Control and Gun Rights*. Westport, CT: Greenwood, 2003.

Wendy Cukier and Victor W. Sidel, *The Global Gun Epidemic: From Saturday Night Specials to AK-47s*. Westport, CT: Praeger Security International, 2006.

Alexander DeConde, *Gun Violence in America: The Struggle for Control*. Boston: Northeastern University Press, 2001.

Tom Diaz, *Making a Killing: The Business of Guns in America*. New York: New Press, 1999.

Jan E. Dizard, Robert Merrill Muth, and Stephen P. Andrews, eds, *Guns in America: A Reader*. New York: New York University Press, 1999.

Arnold Grossman, *One Nation Under Guns: An Essay on an American Epidemic*. Golden, CO: Fulcrum, 2006.

David Hemenway, *Private Guns, Public Health*. Ann Arbor: University of Michigan Press, 2004.

Abigail A. Kohn, *Shooters: Myths and Realities of America's Gun Cultures*. Oxford, UK: Oxford University Press, 2004.

Alan Korwin and Michael P. Anthony, *Gun Laws of America: Every Federal Gun Law on the Books: With Plain English Summaries*. Phoenix, AZ: Bloomfield, 2005.

Wayne LaPierre and James Jay Baker, *Shooting Straight: Telling the Truth About Guns in America*. Washington, DC: Regnery, 2002.

Ted Schwarz, *Kids and Guns: The History, the Present, the Dangers, and the Remedies*. New York: Franklin Watts, 1999.

Michael A. Sommers, *The Right to Bear Arms*. New York: Rosen, 2001.

Robert J. Spitzer, *The Right to Bear Arms: Rights and Liberties under the Law*. Santa Barbara, CA: ABC-CLIO, 2001.

William Weir, *A Well Regulated Militia: The Battle over Gun Control*. North Haven, CT: Archon, 1997.

David C. Williams, The *Mythic Meanings of the Second Amendment: Taming Political Violence in a Constitutional Republic*. New Haven: Yale University Press, 2003.

## Periodicals

Ralph Blumenthal, "Unusual Allies in a Legal Battle over Texas Drivers' Gun Rights," *New York Times*, April 5, 2007.

Diane Cardwell, "Bloomberg Bolsters Gun Drive in Ohio and Kentucky," *New York Times*, April 13, 2007.

———, "City Alleges Illegal Gun Sales in 5 States," *New York Times*, May 16, 2006.

Sewell Chan and Andrew Jacobs, "52 Mayors Unite in Washington to Curb Illegal Firearms," *New York Times*, January 24, 2007.

Laurie P. Cohen and Vanessa O'Connell, "New Legislation Could Scuttle Gun-Crime Suit," *Wall Street Journal*, January 18, 2006.

Ted Cruz, "Second Amendment Showdown," *Wall Street Journal*, March 14, 2007.

Gary Fields and Ryan J. Foley, "Gun Buyers Find Privacy Perk: Bill Would Cut Holding of Records to 24 Hours from 90 Days," *Wall Street Journal*, December 16, 2003.

Jared Flesher and Alexandra Marks, "Should Students Be Allowed to Carry Concealed Weapons?" *Christian Science Monitor*, April 18, 2007.

Mark Fritz, "Selling Guns to the Gun-Shy: To Expand Customer Base, Makers of Firearms Stress Safety, Security and Size," *Wall Street Journal*, July 28, 2005.

Matt Kettmann, "Taking Aim at Hunters' Ammo," *Time*, April 4, 2007.

Dave Kopel, "The U.N. Wants Your Gun," *Wall Street Journal*, July 8, 2006.

Nicholas Kulish and Gary Fields, "'Gun Fingerprinting' Firm Misses Mark—NRA Lobbying Helps to Sow Doubts about Effectiveness of Proposed Ballistics Database," *Wall Street Journal*, November 25, 2002.

Joshua Kurlantzick, "Global Gun Rights?" *New York Times Magazine*, September 17, 2006.

Erich Lichtblau, "Terror Suspects Buying Firearms, U.S. Report Finds," *New York Times*, March 8, 2005.

Carolyn Marshall, "California Bans a Large-Caliber Gun, and the Battle Is On," *New York Times*, January 4, 2005.

*Newsweek* "America Under the Gun," Special Report, August 23, 1999.

*New York Times* "Illinois Ruling Sides with Gun Makers," November 19, 2004.

———, "Robberies and Gun Violence Are Up Despite Crime Drop," September 11, 2006.

———, "Workers' Safety and the Gun Lobby," March 30, 2007.

———, "Eight Years After Columbine," April 17, 2007.

Viveca Novak, "Picking a Fight with the N.R.A.," *Time*, May 31, 1999.

Vanessa O'Connell, "Jury Decides Gun Makers Aren't Liable for Violence," *Wall Street Journal*, May 15, 2003.

Matt Richtel, "San Francisco Gun Vote: Tough Law or Thin?" *New York Times*, November 5, 2005.

Brigid Schulte, "Armed and Determined: Va. Group Openly Carries Guns in Its Effort to Change Laws and Minds," *Washington Post*, November 14, 2004.

Sheryl Gay Stolberg, "Congress Passes New Legal Shield for Gun Industry," *New York Times*, October 21, 2005.

Kevin Sullivan, "Shock, Sympathy and Denunciation of U.S. Gun Laws," *Washington Post Foreign Service*, April 17, 2007.

Dana Thomas, "Americans and Guns," *Newsweek*, June 2002.

Karen Tumulty, "Why No One Shoots Straight on Guns," *Time*, May 26, 2003.

*Wall Street Journal* "Gun Liability Control," July 27, 2005.

———, "Next Debate: Should Colleges Ban Firearms?" April 18, 2007.

*Washington Post* "Court: Gunmakers Not to Blame," November 19, 2004.

Ann Zimmerman, "Wal-Mart to Stop Selling Firearms in Some Stores," *Wall Street Journal*, April 15, 2006.

# Index

## A

Accidents, gun-related, 16–18
Adams, Samuel, 205
*Alston v. United States* (1927), 64
Amar, Akhil, 72, 196, 204, 206,
 207
Amar, Vikram, 196, 204, 206, 207
Annan, Kofi, 98
Anti-gun lobbyists. *See* Gun con-
 trol advocates
*Archives of Pediatric & Adolescent
 Medicine*, 15, 16
ASK ("Asking Saves Kids"), 19
Assault Weapons Control Act
 (AWCA) (1989), 34

## B

Baxley, Frances, 16
*Beretta, Hamilton v. See Hamilton
 v. Beretta* (2001)
Bill of Rights
 applicable to the states, 47–48,
  49, 52
 incorporation of, 33
*The Bill of Rights* (Amar), 72
Bill of Rights guarantees, 44–45,
 46–47
Blackstone, William, 65, 103
Bloomberg, Michael, 147
Bolton, John, 98
Bonanno, Jerry, 97
Boodman, Sandra G., 16
Brady Campaign to Prevent Gun
 Violence, 16
Bureau of Alcohol, Tobacco and
 Firearms (BATF), 122–123, 152

Burger, Warren, 188
Bush, George W., 146
Butler, Bob, 55

## C

California Constitution, 31, 35
California, liability law in, 131,
 132
California Supreme Court, 35
*Cases v. United States* (1942),
 89–90
Centers for Disease Control and
 Prevention (CDC), 15–16
*Central Law Journal*, 46
Child Access Prevention (CAP)
 laws, 16–17
Children and teenagers
 disagreements over gun safety
  for, 19–20
 gun-related deaths of, 14–15
 guns in the home and, 15–16
Children's Defense Fund, 14
*City of New York v. Miln*, 29
Collective rights model of Second
 Amendment
 explained, 99, 101, 172, 190
 in *United States v. Miller*, 86–
  87, 105–106, 190–191
 in *United States v. Emerson*,
  175–177, 198–199
*Commentaries on the Laws of En-
 gland* (Blackstone), 65, 103
Commerce Clause, 169
Constitution, the
 individual rights model of
  Second Amendment and,
  106–109
 on the militia, 64–65

United States v. Emerson (2001) and, 197–198, 201–202

Cruikshank, United States v. (1876), 28, 32–33, 34, 55–56, 57–58

**D**

Dean, David, 145
Deaths, gun-related, 14–16
*Debs v. United States* (1919), 48
Denning, Brannon P., 81
Doctrine of selective incorporation, 32–33
Dorf, Michael C., 187, 197, 198
Douglass, Frederick, 102–103
Dred Scott case, 200–201, 208
Due Process Clause, 32, 168, 169
Duty of care, 120–121, 129–130, 141–143, 143–144, 157–158
Duval, Daniel M., 127

**E**

Eddie Eagle GunSafe Program, 18, 19
Edwards, Timothy Q., 127
Eli Lilly & Co. v. Hymotwitz, 123–124
Emerson, Sacha, 168
Emerson, Timothy, 95, 168, 188–189
*Emerson v. United States. See United States v. Emerson* (2001)
Etzioni, Amitai, 93

**F**

Federal firearms licensees (FFLs), 121
Ferrer, Fernando, 147
Fifteenth Amendment, 201

Fifth Amendment, 36, 168
Fifth Circuit Court of Appeals. *See United States v. Emerson* (2001)
*Firearm Safety in America* (report), 14
First Amendment
  abolition of slavery and, 40–41
  New Deal and, 74–76
Florida, 17
Fourteenth Amendment
  abolition of slavery and, 40
  Bill of Rights guarantees and, 46–47, 49
  Due Process Clause, 32
  *Presser* ruling and, 39, 40
  *United States v. Emerson* decision and, 200–201, 207–208
Fox, Stephen, 113–114, 148
Framers of the Constitution, 107–108
Freedmen's Bureau Act (1866), 207

**G**

Garwood, William, 169
General duty of care, 120–121, 129–130, 141–143, 157–158
Giliberti, Frank J., 138
Ginsburg, Ruth Bader, 178
Golobardes, Mireia Artigot i, 154
Gun Control Act (1968), 37
Gun control advocates
  *Hamilton v. Beretta* and, 135
  intentions of harming gun manufacturers, 136–137, 151
  *Presser* case and, 50, 52, 53–54
  recent setbacks for, 135–136
Gun control, Second Amendment interpretation and, 94–96, 99

Gun manufacturers
  gun opponents' intentions to harm, 136–137
  liability law for, 131–133
  *See also Hamilton v. Beretta* (2001); Lawsuits against gun manufacturers
Gun safety, 16–20
Gun traces, 122–123
Gun violence
  deaths related to, 14–16
  role of negligent manufacturer lawsuits in preventing, 147–148
  safe storage laws and prevention of, 16–18

**H**

Halbrook, Stephen P., 38, 107, 203
Halperin, Edward K., 127
*Hamilton v. Beretta* (2001)
  court decision on, 141–142
  defendants' responsibility and, 140–141
  duty of care and, 129–130
  federal district court's suggestions in, 142
  general duty of care and, 142–143
  gun control advocates and, 135
  inappropriateness of legal liability for manufacturers in, 148
  market share liability and, 130
  overview of, 113–115
  plaintiff evidence needed in, 143–144
  plaintiffs' claims in, 139–140
  state of the law before, 127–128
  Supreme Court decision on, 117–126
  unanswered questions on, 131

Haymarket Riot (1886), 41
Holewinski, Ingrid A., 127
Home, guns in the, 15–16
  attempts to end gun violence and, 19–20
  CAP laws and, 16–18
Hunt, George, 42–43
*Hymowitz v. Eli Lilly & Co.*, 123–124

**I**

Illinois
  gun manufacturer law liability in, 131–132
  law on right to bear arms, 28–29
  military code of, 26–28
Illinois National Guard, 56
*Illinois, Presser v. See Presser v. Illinois* (1886)
Individual rights model of Second Amendment, 81–82, 85–86
  basics of, 101–102
  circumstances surrounding passage of Second Amendment and, 103–104
  as conferred upon "the people," 102–103
  constitutional rationales for, 106–109
  explained, 99, 173, 190
  framing-era history and, 103
  implications of, 109–111
  meaning of "bear arms" and, 178
  *Miller* decision supports, 85–92
  in *United States v. Emerson decision,* 95–96, 169–170, 179–180, 188–189, 192–193, 197

**J**

John Hopkins School of Public Health, 19

**K**

Kates, Don, 91
Kopel, Dave, 50

**L**

Labor struggles, era of, 39, 40, 41, 51
Lawsuits against gun manufacturers, 138–139
    anti-gun lobby's intentions with, 151
    on grounds of negligent entrustment, 158–159
    legislature's vs. court's responsibilities and, 162–163
    market share liability theory and, 159–160
    necessity of liability shield for, 148–149
    on negligence grounds, 139, 157–158
    on nuisance grounds, 160–162
    on products liability grounds, 156
    responsibility of retailers and, 152–153
    role in gun violence prevention, 147–148
    unsuccessful, 154–155
    *See also Hamilton v. Beretta* (2001); Protection of Lawful Commerce in Arms Act (2005)
Layton, Frank, 60, 63, 105
Legislation on child access to guns, 16–17
    *See also* Protection of Lawful Commerce in Arms Act (2005); State gun control legislation

Lehr und Wehr Verein military company, 22, 51, 57
Levinson, Stanford, 71–72, 73
*Lewis v. United States* (1980), 192
Liability lawsuits, 138–139, 152
    *See also* Lawsuits against gun manufacturers
Libertarian approach to Second Amendment. *See* Individual rights model of Second Amendment
*Linder v. United States* (1925), 64

**M**

MacKenzie, Frederick, 206
*MacPherson v. Buick Motor Co.* (1916), 129
Madison, James, 137
Manufacturers, civil litigation involving, 138–139, 152
    *See also* Lawsuits against gun manufacturers
Market share liability, 115, 130
    background information on, 123–124
    before *Hamilton,* 128
    in *Hamilton* vs. other liability cases, 124–125
    lawsuits against gun manufacturers and, 159–160
Marketing, negligent, 138–139
    *See also Hamilton v. Beretta* (2001)
McClendon, Regina, 30
McReynolds, James Clark, 60, 62, 85–86
Military Code of Illinois, 26–28
Militia
    collective rights interpretation of Second Amendment and, 101
    meaning of, in Second Amendment, 199, 205

in *Miller* decision, 60–61, 64–68

in *Presser* case, 23, 25–26, 42–43, 55–56, 57–58

Miller, Jack, 60, 63, 77–78, 105

Miller, Matthew, 16, 19

*Miller, United States v. See* United States v. Miller (1939)

Moral function of the Second Amendment, 109

*Muscarello v. United States* (1998), 178

**N**

National Association for the Advancement of Colored People (NAACP), 148–149

National Firearms Act (1934)

*Miller* case and, 60, 63–64, 74, 78, 174–175

New Deal and, 76

privilege against self-incrimination and, 36

regulation of machine guns and, 88–89

National Guard, 41, 56

National Rifle Association (NRA)

on gun-related deaths among children, 14–15

on safe storage laws, 18

support from the courts for, 95

Negligence lawsuits. *See* Lawsuits against gun manufacturers

Negligent entrustment doctrine, 121–122, 128, 131, 143, 158–159

Negligent marketing

is only a theory, 144

law protecting gun manufacturers accused of, 146–147

situations involving manufacturer duty of care and, 143–144

*See also* Lawsuits against gun manufacturers

New Deal, 74–76

New York Court of Appeals, 141–143

*Nigro v. United States* (1928), 64

Nuisance, lawsuits against gun manufacturers on grounds of, 160–162

**P**

Parker, Robert M., 169, 183

Pennsylvania Constitution of 1776, 194

Pennsylvania Declaration of Rights (1776), 204

Pennsylvania, market share liability and, 132–133

*Plessy v. Ferguson* (1896), 47

Pratt, Erich, 134

Preemption, state gun control legislation and, 36–37

Presser, Herman, 22, 57

*Presser v. Illinois* (1886), 22–58

acknowledgment of right to gun ownership in, 53–54

analysis of, 46

anti-gun lobbyist interpretation of, 50

arming the militia and, 55–56

Bill of Rights guarantees and, 46–47

contemporary views of, 47–49

current implications of, 52

historical context for, 51, 56

history of labor conflict and, 40

individual right to bear arms and, 32–33

legacy of, 39–40

limits on state gun laws and, 52–53

overview of, 22–23, 57

right to assemble and, 44–45

Supreme Court decision on, 24–29, 42–44, 51–52

validity of nonincorporation and, 33, 34

*Printz v. United States* (1997), 72

Privilege against self-incrimination, 36

*Protect Children, Not Guns 2007* (report), 14

Protection of Lawful Commerce in Arms Act (2005), 115

benefits of, 165

concerns raised over, 146–149, 165–166

Congress was justified in passing, 151–153

exceptions holding gun industry liable, 164–165

as providing immunity to the gun industry, 163–164

purpose of, 155

Public nuisance, 160–162

**R**

Ragon, Heartsill, 60

Rebman, Alethea K., 127

Reese, Charley, 150

Registration of weapons, 36

Rendell, Edward, 136

Revisionist position

on the Second Amendment, 71–72, 73–74, 87–88

on *United States v. Miller,* 78–79

Reynolds, Glenn H., 81

Right to assemble

Cruikshank case and, 57–58

labor movement and, 41

in *Presser* case, 44–45

workers' organizations and, 51

Right to keep and bear arms

belongs to everyone, 137

California Constitution on, 35

founding era documents on meaning of, 193–194

gun control advocates on, 137

individual vs. state right approach to, 31–35

international community and, 98

in the *Miller* decision, 67–69

in the *Presser* case, 22–23, 28–29, 42–43, 43, 51

state application of, 39–40

*See also* Second Amendment; *United States v. Emerson* (2001)

**S**

Safe storage laws, 16–18

Scalia, Antonin, 178

Scarry, Elaine, 77

Second Amendment, 206

abolition of slavery and, 40–41

circumstances surrounding passage of, 103–104

debate on, 71, 99

differing interpretations of, 72–74, 99, 172–173, 189–190

gun control measures are supported by interpretation of, 94–96

the historical vs. contemporary, 199–200

incorporation of, 33

later Amendments altering meaning of, 200–201

meaning of, 99–100

meaning of "bear arms" in, 177–178

meaning of "keep...arms" in, 179

meaning of "militia" in, 199

meaning of "the people" in, 137, 177, 199, 205–206

in *Miller* decision, 60, 74, 77–78, 85–86, 104–106

Miller decision supports individual rights model of, 86–92

misplaced debate over nature of, 184–186

need for defending, 153

under the New Deal, 76

possible readings of, 77

preamble of, 193

*Presser* case and, 52

reasons for arming and, 206–207

response to the Standard Model of, 82–84

revisionist position on, 71–72

state gun laws and, 52–53

substantive guarantee in, 179–180

twenty-first century meaning of, 194–195

in *United States v. Emerson* decision, 168, 169–170, 172, 175–177, 180–182

*See also* Collective rights model of Second Amendment; Right to keep and bear arms; individual rights model of Second Amendment

Self-defense, safe storage laws and, 17–18

Self-preservation function of the Second Amendment, 107–109

Sherman, Roger, 207

*Silveira v. Lockyer*, 96

Slavery, abolition of, 40–41

*Sonzinsky v. United States* (1937), 64

Souter, David H., 178

*Spies v. United States* (1943), 48

Standard model. *See* individual rights model of Second Amendment

State gun control legislation

arguments against, 35–37

limitations on, in *Presser* case and, 43–44, 51, 52–53

objections to, 31

Second Amendment restricts authority to enact, 188

"State Gun Safe Storage Laws and Child Mortality Due to Firearms" (study), 17

State power

Fourteenth Amendment and, 46–47

right to assemble and, 44–45

Story, Allan C., 22, 42, 46

**T**

Tenth Amendment, 106, 169

Texas, 132

*That Every Man Be Armed: The Evolution of a Constitutional Right* (Halbrook), 107

Thomas, Clarence, 72

Tracing of guns, 122–123

Trumbull, Lyman, 22, 42

**U**

United Nations Conference on the Illicit trade in Small Arms and Light Weapons in all Its Aspects, 98

*United States v. Cruikshank* (1876), 28, 32–33, 34, 55–56, 57–58

*United States v. Doremus* (1919), 64

*United States v. Emerson* (2001), 72

collective right interpretation of Second Amendment in, 175–177, 198–199

concurring opinion in, 184–186

the Constitution and, 197–198

court's decision on, 172–182

*Dred Scott* case cited in, 200–201, 208

focused on the 1789 Constitutional text, 201–202

Fourteenth Amendment and, 200–201, 207–208

individual rights interpretation of Second Amendment and, 95–96, 169–170, 179–180, 192–193

meaning of "bear arms" and, 198, 204–205

meaning of "militia" in, 205

meaning of "the people" in, 205–206

overview of, 168–169, 188–189

*United States v. Miller* and, 190–192

*United States v. Jin Fuey Moy* (1916), 64

*United States v. Miller* (1939), 34

collective rights interpretation of Second Amendment in, 86–87, 105–106, 190–192

endorses an individual rights model of the Second Amendment, 86–92

overview of, 60–61

reasons behind the Courts' readings of, 79–80

rejection of Second Amendment challenge in, 74, 77–78

revisionists' view of, 78–79

Second Amendment treatment in, 104–106

Supreme Court's decision on, 62–69, 84–86

**V**

Validity of nonincorporation, 33–34

Vernick, Jon, 19

Violence Against Women Act, 158

**W**

Waldrop, Tanya, 127

*Wealth of Nations* (Smith), 65–66

Weinstein, Jack B., 161

Wesley, Richard C., 116

Williams, David, 77

Woods, William Burnham, 24, 43–44

**Y**

Yassky, David, 70, 82–84, 87–92